Remember

By

Quest Delaney

Remember Copyright © 2019 by Quest Delaney. All rights reserved.

No part of this publication may be reproduced, stored in a retrieval system or transmitted in any way by any means, electronic, mechanical, photocopy, recording or otherwise without the prior permission of the author except as provided by USA copyright law.

Acknowledgments

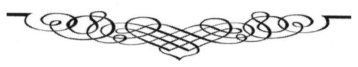

To my Lord and Savior, Jesus Christ. Without Him I couldn't share my experiences with you. Thank you, God, for allowing me to see heaven.

To my wonderful Mother. Your strength lives in me. A mother is a gift given from God. I am so thankful to have such a beautiful mother. I love you, Ma, from the bottom of my heart! Thank you so much for giving birth to me. For forty years of my life, you've taught me to be strong. You've always inspired me. You would say, "Remember where you came from, so you know where you are going. Understand there are times you must admit defeat, and start all over, building anew. You must visualize success. Never think or say, "I can't!" Just believe in yourself, and you'll be blessed to conquer obstacles that stand in your way." I have learned and I'm still learning the wonders of life. Thank you from the bottom of my heart for building such an artistic mind of creativity. My spiritual mind has blossomed to such new levels. I now understand what you meant. What a wonderful combination!

To my dearest Father. God placed you in my mother's life. It was the love you shared with her that created me. Without your creativity and your artistic abilities, my vision wouldn't have been clear to me at all. Thanks for your love, Pops! Much love to you. Thank you, Mom and Dad. To my beautiful sister, Ty. You are my world! Without you my spirit wouldn't be the same. We've done everything together since we were three years old. We are completely in sync with one another. When I look in the mirror, I not only see me, but you, too! Our love for each other is nothing short of heaven. No one comes closer. You're my beautiful sister and my best friend.

Acknowledgments

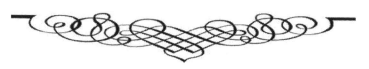

To my beautiful children, Devin and Quest, and Kayla: I love you from my heart. I enjoy being your father.

To my sisters and brothers, Apria, O'Shea, Cierra, and Sabian, I couldn't ask for a much happier family. I love you all with my heart and soul.

To my wonderful nephew and niece, J'Waun and Tyshiya: Your mother's passing and going to heaven is something very special. She allowed me to come with her and now I can share that moment with the whole world. Her love lives on through our family and the people she touched. There's nothing in the world I wouldn't do for you. You've lost a wonderful mother who gave birth to you. So, please, enjoy life to the fullest because that's what she would have wanted. When you're lonely, just call your mother for guidance. She loved you both so much.

All my love and many thanks to the Delaney's, Gallman's, Boyd's, Tripline's, Harrison's, and the Norwood's.

Love is the most beautiful feeling and it is something that you can give to someone special. Tomorrow is not promised. Please love with your whole heart. I always do. Thank you so much for touching my life and my heart. I hope you enjoy what

I wrote because I've poured my heart out on every page, some more than others. I pray that you are blessed.

My greatest appreciation and love goes to my family, but especially to my mother and sister. I'm honored to be loved by you. Without you my heart would be lonely. Your love is so special to me. I thank God every day for you being in my life.

Sending My love:

The First Baptist Church of Glenarden family, Pastor John K. Jenkins, Sr., Rev. Sims, Pastor Duane E. Dickens, Sr., and Minister Billy T. Staton, Jr. and their families. Without your love and belief, this book would have never been possible.

Special love to Kenny Loggins's for the song "Love Will Follow," which was playing while I wrote this book. Your song means a lot to my heart.

To BeBe and Cee Cee Wynans, your song, "Heaven" speaks to my heart so dearly. My little sister and I loved singing this song together so many times.

To Michael Jackson, whom I love dearly. This book was written before your death. Because of the love and emotion on "Never Can Say Good-bye" and "Got To Be There," they were something special that I would play for my little sister while she was falling asleep. I had no idea that those two songs would mean so much to me.

To the whole world, tell someone you care about that you love 'em.

Much Love World, from Quest Delaney…

Table of Contents

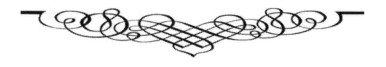

Preface..12

Introduction...13

My Experience..16

The Phone Call...34

I Must be Dreaming..37

The Waiting Room..43

Feeling Numb...47

The Blueprint..51

She's Alive..53

Spirit to Spirit...55

Is There a Heaven?...58

Her Smile..59

To Keisha..62

Mad at God..63

My Little Sister Talking...............................66

Paradise..74

Tricks in the Air...79

Angel Clouds...81

Welcome Back...84

We enter Heaven..86

What "Quest" Means..................................91

Paradise Wings..95

Roses that Love.......................................100

The Kingdom...103

Inside the Palace......................................106

The Love of an Angel...............................108

Devine Guidance......................................116

I Believe..121

At the Table...123

The Teaching Begins................................125

Mom, I Have Something to Tell You..........128

Lost Without my Sister..132

Ask for an Angel...135

One Last Tear...138

Surprise Me...142

Three Crosses..146

Her Presence...148

Questions People Ask Me...152

What is the Book of Life?...154

Trying to Move On...157

Dad..163

Mother...167

My Grandmother..172

A Star...175

Saved by an Angel..179

Frisbee...182

My First Out of Body Experience................................191

Invisible..200

Mirror..206

My Spiritual Dream..208

Preface

To have a little sister is the most wonderful feeling in the world. It's a special gift from God. I still have so much love for her. My heart will never be the same without her! Her love will live forever for those whom she touched with her heart.

Introduction

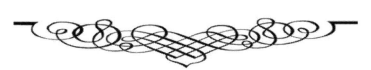

My passion and drive to write this book stems from my desire to help others who have suffered a traumatic brain injury or any type of trauma or medical condition that causes memory loss. Any type of injury that makes one forget about who they are, who their loved ones are, how to love, and how to express love, leaving them with only the pain of the injury and the loss of their natural senses can understand how life changing it is to know that you are not alone, and even better to know that there are people out there who have walked through the same experience. Not knowing how to move forward in your life from that type of injury leaves you feeling helpless. It is utterly debilitating to wake up and not know who you are, not to recognize yourself in the mirror, but it's even worse when you realize that you are in your 40's and you don't remember any of the things you've learned and lived up to that point. Realizing that you don't feel anything, not knowing how or if you will ever feel any emotion again is surreal and frightening. Realizing that you don't even know what love is, or whether or not you will ever be able to feel love anymore, or know how to express love, or joy, just pain and loss makes suicidal thoughts your constant companion, but in spite of the horror of it all, the one anchoring thought after losing my memory, was the memory of my journey to heaven with my sister. God stepped in and allowed me to hang on to that single memory. It was the one single experience that I clung to like it was the only memory of my life because it was, until God started to show me how to rebuild the memories of my life, I had no hope. The beauty of this experience though was the joy of realizing that God was helping me put my life back together, only this time, it was like I was seeing it all for the first time and this time, it seemed so much better. God allowed me to experience my life, as if I was a passenger observing someone else's life. It was as if my eyes were showing my brain who I was all over again. I can't even explain what it felt like to watch your life looking at it from the perspective of a passenger. It was disorienting to say the least. God told me to keep my faith and my belief in tact and, as a result, he would restore everything that I lost, and it was truly that promise that kept me on this side of life, it was the only thing that made me want to keep living. With each day, God has blessed me to learn who I am all over again, as if He was intentionally molding me into the man that He intended me to be. I feel so amazed, humbled, and overwhelmed with so much gratitude for my life, for my family, my friends, and loved ones. I am rediscovering talents and abilities that I used to have before the injury and even becoming familiar with and discovering new talents and abilities. I am still healing and there is still so much more for God to show me about my life and who I truly am, but I feel better equipped now to take the journey then I probably was before the accident because everything feels new. I look forward to the new day now and I am excited and empowered to create the life that I have always wanted.

Understanding now how significant the memory of my sister's passing and the brief journey we took to heaven together was to me at the time of my injury, makes me have a deeper appreciation of how important it is to have hope when you are faced with such tragedy. Experiencing the significance of hope compels me to want to just reach out to everyone suffering in any way and shower the gift of love through hope. Hope was truly my anchor and I just want to encourage anyone who has experienced the loss of someone close to them passing away suddenly, no matter if it was your mother, father, grandparents, brother, sister, uncle, aunt, spouse, significant other or friend to hang on to the hope that life brings. Life will certainly be different without them, but hanging on to hope that there is a life, though a different one, God can and will restore your life in ways that only He can and when you get to the other side you will truly have a deeper appreciation for everything and everyone that makes up your life.

For me, when my sister passed, God blessed me with the gift of spending the day with her as she made the journey to heaven. Can you imagine what it would feel like to have them come back to you for a day? Would you love them even more?

Love makes the heart smile, so tell that someone who means the world to you, "I love you so much." Maybe that person is going through problems, had a hard day, or just wants to hear those beautiful words. Always be willing to love from deep within.

For it is within where love and hope will bloom.

My Experience

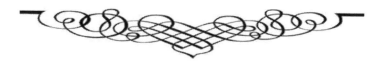

January 7, 2015, it was like any other day. 4:00 a.m., the alarm goes off, it's time to get up and go to work. I went to look out the window to see if it had snowed, and it hadn't, but I sure wanted to stay home. It had snowed days before, so I was hoping I got snowed in, but I had to get ready to head in anyway. On my way in every day, I always listen to "The Morning Word", a radio show that gives the audience positive things to meditate on. So, I'm getting my daily dose in and I'm riding down the highway feeling good. As I pull into the parking lot, spaces were limited because there was so much snow, and at first I thought I was going to have to park in another lot and have to walk through the snow, but suddenly, someone puts their headlights on and pulls out the parking lot and I thought, "FAVOR!", yes, now I could just park and be close to the building. I got out of the truck and started walking toward the building for roll call. I took the same path I always take up to the gear up room where all the officers check their weapons and ensure they have adequate ammunition. Roll call is over, so I hook up with my partner and we start walking toward our starting location. While we were getting there, we were having general conversation about what's on the agenda for the day and during the conversation, my partner slips on an icy patch and almost loses his balance, but he doesn't fall. It shocked us both and the first thing I said to him was, "Boy! If you would have fell.......", and before I could finish my sentence I slipped, fell, and my head went slamming into the concrete. I blacked out for a few minutes, and my partner shook me to try and bring me back around, he checked my pulse, but I was really out of it. As I started to come to, I realized that my left foot was under me making it difficult for me to get up. I noticed that my left hand was beneath me and it made it even harder for me to get up so when I tried, I slipped again and the left side of my head hit the ground again and the next thing you know, I'm sliding down the street pretty hard toward the bottom of the hill. Luckily, my partner was there to keep me from sliding any further. As I got up, I didn't realize that my left ankle was fractured, all I knew is that it hurt. My partner reached out for me to grab his hand, but for some reason, I didn't realize I was on the ground so as I reached for his hand, I thought he was trying to dap me up and shake my hand. I was experiencing some double vision so as I went to grab his hand, I missed several times because I was pretty disoriented. My partner grabbed me to help me keep my balance because I was having a hard time getting my footing. As I stood up again, I went to tie my boot back up tighter. I felt weird, but I tried to shake it off. As my partner was asking me if I was ok, it just seemed like he was speaking in slow motion.

As we walked to our destination, the EMT's were called,

they arrive at the scene to assess me. The EMT's went on to examine me by asking more questions and as I was responding, I could hear one of my previous academy corporals saying, "Are you in pain? Are you injured?", a few reasons for this is to determine if a person can block out some of the pain and keep moving through the day. Even with my trying to block out the pain, I still felt like something was off because it seemed like everyone was moving and talking slowly. I realized that it wasn't them moving and talking slowly, it was me

I worked for a couple of more hours and wanted to work more, but I realized that my observation skills were impaired, and I couldn't focus I even noticed that I started to jumble my words. Once I realized what was happening, I felt fear. Fear of not being able to perform my duties because I started being consumed about all of the "what if's". I brought my concerns up immediately to my sergeant's attention and at that moment, we called the EMT's again. EMT came out to assess me again and this time, they suggested that I go to the hospital, they specifically said to "clock out, go to the hospital, and go home". I guess my pride took over, and I made the decision to drive myself home instead. I actually engaged the GPS to get home even though I wouldn't normally do that.

As I started driving, I started thinking about so many things, it was almost like my life was flashing before me and those thoughts just kept repeating in my mind. It was like my spirit was telling me, "I love you…always believe in your dreams…", they were random thoughts just repeating in my head. I realized that I was approaching a bridge that I was familiar with since childhood and as I passed, I saw two people standing there. I couldn't understand why they were just standing there or why I was so fixated on them. As I passed them, I turned forward to pay attention to the road, then looked back again and they were gone. "There's no way! I thought………

NO WAY they walked off the bridge that fast". I didn't realize it then what the meaning of me seeing those people on the bridge was all about at the time, but I'll revisit that in later chapters.

After the bridge, as I was driving home, I recall feeling really warm and tingly inside. By the time I reached my house, I realized that I don't remember even driving home. What I did know is that I just kept praying, "God just please get me home safely". I wasn't panicked, I wasn't scared, I was calm, it was like I blacked out and then suddenly realized I was home, but I couldn't tell you how I got there. All I know is that I got there safely. I knew without a shadow of a doubt that it was only God's grace and probably some guardian angels that got me home that day because I literally do not know how I made it. I don't remember the drive, all I remember was seeing those people on the bridge. As I got out of the truck, I just staring at everything looking around like I knew I was home, but there was a sense of unfamiliarity. I knew I drove, and I knew I was home, but everything felt like an echo. I started feeling unfamiliar with everything I was looking at and random thoughts started coming into my mind like, as I stared at the stairs, I instantly felt that I would have an issue with getting up the stairs for some reason. I was thinking to myself; I know this is where I live, but is this really where I live? Everything started to really feel unfamiliar and I was becoming very disoriented. It was the weirdest feeling I had ever felt, and I normally would never question myself or feel uncertain about where home is. When I got to the front door about to go inside, I looked at my keys and couldn't figure out what key was the house key! I knew for sure that something was wrong, and I was in trouble. As I walked in, even the inside of my house looked different. I started feeling anxiety because I had never felt this uncertain. I thought taking a shower would help, so I did, and I was just relaxing on the couch, waiting for my girlfriend at the time to get home from work. When she finally walked in, it felt like I didn't even know her!?!?! I felt myself staring at her because I didn't recognize her, and I chalked it up to just being tired. I had already called her when I was at the job to tell her what had happened, so when she walked in the house, she was ready to go to the hospital. As we left the house, the same stair case I came up suddenly looked like a roller coaster, I started thinking about falling, and I started to get even more anxious which was completely outside of my normal character. Then I don't even remember getting down the stairs, I just remember saying to her, "Dang, these are some seriously steep steps!". I think at that moment, she realized that something serious was going on with me and that I might be feeling the effects of being more seriously injured than either of us first imagined.

As we drove to the hospital, I remember her telling me, "Just put your head back and relax yourself", which is normally what I always used to say to other people. I suddenly started feeling my heartbeat pounding in my head, it was beating so hard; it felt like my head was going to pop off of my shoulders! My eyes were throbbing to the beat of my heart so that it felt like they were going to pop out of my head too! At the time, we lived very close to the hospital, maybe five minutes at that, but it seemed like we had been driving for an hour. As we pulled up to the hospital, I told her that I felt like I couldn't really move and that's when she asked me, "Do we need to get you some help to get out of the truck? Or a wheelchair?", and I said, "No, we don't need a wheelchair, I can do it". As I got out of the truck, my whole body was hurting, my hands were tingling and numb, my neck was hurting, my back, and my left ankle were all hurting. I thought to myself that it felt like I just got hit by a truck.

When we checked into the emergency room, I just remember the receptionist asking me my name and I had to pause for a minute; it took me a bit to respond to the question because I had to really think about it. When the doctor finally called me back, I explained the accident to them an told them all of the symptoms I was experiencing, they evaluated me and explained that I had a concussion with a hematoma and multiple other injuries and that I needed to just go home and rest and be off from work until I stopped feeling those symptoms. Five years later, after the accident, I am still recovering. As we left the hospital to go home, I'm starting to feel my mind really drifting. Trees started to look like dinosaurs, and I found myself thinking about how trees could grow that big? I didn't realize that my memory was really starting to fail. Then, I looked over at my girlfriend and thought, "Wow, ok, this is my girlfriend? Ok, this is my girlfriend, but why is she driving me?". I didn't realize that my injury was starting to make me feel more and more confused and that my mind was pondering the smallest things, all of a sudden. I was like a puppy putting his head out of the car window for the first time, it was like everything was new. When we went to the hospital it was still daylight, but as we drove home, it was night time and I couldn't account for all of the time that passed and I suddenly started feeling anxious because my mind just kept wondering why is this, why that, why, why, why??? I couldn't believe that the injury was starting to have such a negative impact on me already. It was starting to get scary for me and to this day, I have the same anxiety when I hear the word "why"; it doesn't matter if someone else says it to me or if I'm thinking it to myself, but I especially hate when I hear it in my head because the feeling of confusion and the thought of my not knowing something that I should know or I may have known in the past almost drove me to the point of insanity during my recovery.

 The more we drove and the closer we got to home, the more I started not recognizing the way home. By the time we got there, I had completely lost any recognition of home and as I watched her get out of the truck, I had to pause and watch her because I couldn't remember how to open the door to get out of the truck, so she had to help me. Normally, I would get out and get to the door first to unlock the door for her, but this time, I looked at the stairs in fear because I was feeling overwhelmed as to why the stairs were so high. I asked myself, "Why are the stairs made like this?". She asked me if I needed help going up the stairs because I was hesitant as we approached them and I said, "Yes". I hate admitting it, but I was afraid to walk up the stairs, all I could think about is that they were going to collapse. I felt myself sweating like I was running a marathon. There was something in me that was changing.

I never had anxiety before in my life, but I was experiencing it for the first time and with each moment it was growing. We made it up the stairs, but when I looked back down at them, I got nauseous because they looked so high. When we made it inside, I completely had forgotten everything... I was intrigued at the fish tank we had because all I could think about is how do fish breathe underwater? This was getting ridiculous and I felt so many emotions inside of me; I wanted to cry from the frustration of what was happening to me right before my eyes, I felt helpless. I was unable to do anything like articulate a sentence, to ask for help, or to tell her what was happening to me. It was like I wanted to say something but for some reason I couldn't think of the words. I found myself spacing off and catching myself mumbling in response to questions as a matter of fact, I hate to say this now, but I realized that I didn't even know her name. I got very upset about not remembering her name and having a difficult time thinking of the words to express it. I grabbed a pen and paper thinking that maybe the words would come to me if I focused on writing it down. I felt the tears welling up in my eyes, so I went into the bathroom to give myself some privacy and I started writing down my emotions and what I was feeling in hopes that it might give her some idea of what was happening to me.

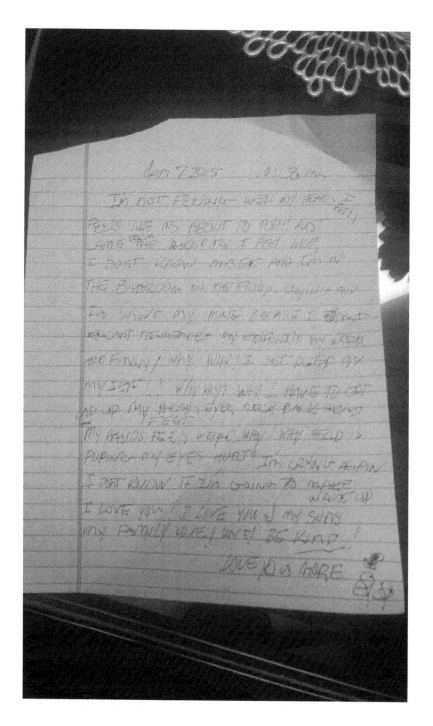

After I wrote the letter, I put it away but as I was writing, it really felt like I wasn't going to survive this. Now that I look at the letter almost five years later, I can tell that there were a lot of things that were "off". My penmanship was off, my sentence structure was off, everything about me at that time was slightly off. It makes me emotional every time to think about myself following during the experience. I don't think any of us knew or were prepared at the time for the reality that I was experiencing a full-blown traumatic brain injury. The reality was I looked fine on the outside, but blank stares can mean stroke, or not being responsive to simple questions, like, "What do you want to eat?", for a person with a traumatic brain injury that can be like riding a bike with no chain and you can't stop while going down a hill with no brakes. If someone told me to use my feet to stop the bike, I wouldn't be able to comprehend why they would make that suggestion because I wasn't able to comprehend how my feet would stop the bike. It felt so overwhelming, and I just felt more and more exhausted to the point that all I wanted to do was sleep. So, I laid down on the sofa for a few hours.

A few hours later, she came to check on me and I remember she kissed my forehead. When I woke up, I got up only to go lay back down in the bedroom., however She had to take me because I didn't remember where it was. I laid down again and woke up a few more hours later, yet this time I woke up even more disoriented and I had to use the restroom. I looked over and she was asleep, and I just remember wondering, where am I? Who was this lady in my bed? What is going on right now? I had to go to the bathroom, but I didn't want to wake her let her know that I needed to go to the bathroom, let alone didn't know where the bathroom was, I was completely disoriented. Luckily the bathroom was right next to the bedroom, but I couldn't distinguish the bathroom from the kitchen, I just remember thinking, "where do I go?". I had held it for so long that I started to go so I grabbed the toilet seat, pulled it up, sat down and let it go! I didn't even turn the light on because I didn't know I needed to turn on the light and when I got done, I didn't know I was supposed to flush the toilet. I went to leave the bathroom and I grabbed the wall and hit the light switch and it was as if it was the first time I had ever encountered a light, so I sat there and played with it for a minute, turning it on, and off, and on, and off. All I could think to myself was, "how is that happening?", then I see a shoulder in the mirror in my peripheral vision which makes me jump back because I thought some- one else was in the bathroom. I jumped back to hide, but then I wanted to see who that was, so I moved back toward the mirror not realizing that it was a mirror, but only because I wanted to see who was in the bathroom with me and suddenly, I saw myself and it scared me. I didn't recognize myself and I didn't know it was my reflection and I started to punch out the mirror from the shock. I shouted, "Who the hell is that?" loud enough to have woke my girlfriend. I went back into the bedroom to lay down and try and go back to sleep, I closed my eyes and tried to get comfortable, but I just couldn't fall back to sleep because I was so disturbed about not having recognized myself in the mirror. I wound up crying myself to sleep. I woke back up again when it was time for her to get up, but I still didn't recognize who she was. I noticed that she had gone into the bathroom to get ready for the day and I just found myself staring at her. I waited for her to come back out of the bathroom and when she opened the door again, she was brushing her teeth, which may as well have been the first time I'd ever seen it, and she asked me if I was ok. I didn't know how to respond so I just said, "ok, um, hmm…". As she walked around the house getting ready for work, I found myself following her like a lost puppy. I kept wanting to express myself and tell her that I didn't recognize her, but I couldn't figure out how to say it to her, so everything she asked me was like the first time I had ever heard it. I started feeling emotional again, so I sat down on the sofa to gather my thoughts. I started feeling overwhelmed with emotion again at the frustration of not being able to communicate. I felt like she was leaving me, even though she was only going to work, but I couldn't help but feel completely helpless and it made me cry again, but I was careful to wipe my tears before she came back in the room. As she started to walk toward the door to go to work, I followed her. I was feeling hysterical, but instead of telling her how I was feeling, I broke down instead. She was consoling me and telling me that she was only going in for a couple of hours, but I just recall feeling like she was leaving forever. She kissed me goodbye and told me that she loved me, and I responded with the same thing to her, but I really didn't remember exactly what that even meant, it just seemed right to say those words back to her. I closed the door and I lost it. I watched her get in her truck and drive away and it left me feeling devastated. After watching her leave I went back to the door because I felt like chasing after her, but as soon as I saw those stairs, I was terrified because I was reminded how I had forgotten how to go up and down the stairs, so I came back in the house and just yelled, "WHY? WHY ME?" with tears streaming down my face and I felt so alone because I didn't understand that she would return later. I went to the balcony as if I would see her, but I knew she had just drove away. I stood there cold, frustrated, and disoriented and didn't even know how to warm myself up. As I stood on the balcony, a part of me was saying that I should just jump off the balcony, then shortly afterward, I heard another voice telling me that it wasn't a good idea. It made me have thoughts about suicide to even imagine living my life in that state for the rest of my life. When I finally came back in from the balcony I was disoriented, confused, and terrified about the condition of my mind.

    I came in, closed the door, and sat there in the same spot all day looking out of the window like a dog waiting for his master to return home. She would call through-out the day to check on me, but when I got up to answer the phone, I was confused about how to actually connect to her call so it took a few times for me to figure I out how to do that. I finally answered and I was so excited and happy to hear her voice. The only words I remember where the words she said to me, so I said, "I love you". I was thinking that the more she spoke, the more I would be able to rely on her to drive the conversation because I really couldn't figure out how to string words together to express anything. After she asked me how I was doing and realized that I really didn't know how to communicate how I was doing, we hung up the phone.

    After hanging up the phone, I felt emotional all over again.

The way I dealt with it was to have suicidal thoughts and as I blinked my eyes, it was like someone was trying to transmit images or scenes from a movie in my head because I kept having these visions of heaven. From that day on, every time I experienced anything negative, I would get these vivid flashes of heaven and as time passed, the flashes of heaven became clearer and clearer, and I would sometimes see my little sister Keisha and when that would happen, it would make me feel so calm, happy, and at peace. Every time it happened; it was the one thing that I was certain I had experienced. I struggled to find the words to express that I was experiencing the visions and the fact that they were happening to me quite frequently. Each time the visions would get more and more vivid with each experience.

With each day that my girlfriend would come home, I felt like I was getting happier and more excited to see her, especially since I would feel so alone when she was gone. I really wanted to share about the memories I was recalling, but I just couldn't find the words to express myself. So, this went on for months because I just didn't know how to express to her that this was happening. Finally, as I started to recall my day to day activities, my not being able to clearly express my emotions just became a frustration that I lived with every day, and the loneliness grew inside of both of us. I believe that it created distance that wasn't there before, but again, I just could never put the words together to express it. One day, I was meditating, and I was having a conversation with God and I explicitly heard him tell me to get a dog. It seemed to come out of the blue and when I processed that, I expressed to God how broken I felt I was, and that if I couldn't remember, if I couldn't express myself, if I couldn't recall memories or how to put words together, how to brush my teeth, how to taste, smell or any of those basic abilities, how could I possibly handle the responsibility of a pet? I felt like I had turned into some shell of myself and here God was asking me to get a dog? It just seemed crazy at the time. I felt angry at God because I know that He allowed this to happen to me and how am I supposed to get a dog and how is that going to help me get back on track? He told me that the dog was going to help me fill the place of love that you have lost. I didn't understand at the time how that was going to help me get healed, but I was open.

When my girlfriend came home, I was excited to make the suggestion to her, so when she walked in the door, I said, "We should get a dog!", and she looked at me with this really puzzled look. I didn't know how or if I should have even mentioned to her that God spoke to me, because I didn't want her to think I was crazy and of course, I didn't know how to express it to her or how to explain it to her. She was shocked that I wanted to get a dog then with all that I was going through at the time, but she was open, and we eventually got one. So, we got Jazz, a Shitzu- Bijon mix and he really brought me a lot of happiness, joy, and love to me. Go figure, God was right again! Of course. The dog gave me the ability to have feelings and emotions again and it was wonderful to feel that unconditional love, it opened me up again from all of the anger and frustration that I had been feeling from the accident. I still had progress to make, but it allowed me to open up another aspect of myself that I feel was closed after the accident. I wasn't the same person that I was before the accident and that really caused a lot of challenges in our relationship.

I truly began to feel more and more alone and that made me feel like shutting down. My lack of ability to communicate created more and more stress on me and on the relationship and that began to cause depression, headaches, and disruptions in my sleep patterns, which led to my needing more and more medicines that helped me deal with the pain and frustration. I started to slip into a very dark place. I felt like the man that I was actually died after the accident and I hated who I became. The anxiety of the relationship issues with my girlfriend intensified and I continued to feel lonelier and more inadequate and it sent me into a tailspin of pain and anguish that one day, I overmedicated and God saved me helping me get to the hospital without incident. I admitted myself to the hospital and I am constantly hearing this phone ringing, and as I was sitting there totally out of it, I heard my sister Keisha's voice say, "It's going to be ok Big Brother". Hearing that really made me breakdown and cry right there in the lobby of the emergency room and the nurse came and asked me if I was ok, and for the first time since the accident, I was able to express, "No, I'm not ok". I started having flashes of Keisha and I in heaven and it was almost like those flashes were keeping me awake. As I began to slouch down in the chair, the nurse became concerned enough to have someone come and get me and put me in a wheelchair and moved to a bed.

As we moved to a room in the back with a bed, I was having negative thoughts like, "You should just die", and with each of those thoughts, I started to get flashes of when I visited heaven with my sister Keisha. It was as if there was a battle going on in my soul and I was feeling the pressure of making the decision to live or die. As I drifted in and out of coherence, I kept hearing, "Remember" and seeing flashes of the experience I had when I visited heaven with my sister. Soon they started to flash faster and faster like scenes to a movie, and I kept hearing a phone ringing, I didn't know where that sound was coming from, but exhausted by the whole over-medicating, they ended up keeping me overnight at the hospital and shortly after being admitted, I finally drifted off to sleep in the safety of the medical professionals.

When I awoke the next morning, I hadn't felt that good in months following the accident. I awoke clear, refreshed, and almost renewed! It was as if I had just passed through the eye of the needle and made it through to the other side of a very bad journey. The most amazing part of that experience though, was that when I woke up, I could remember every detail of the spiritual experience I had with my sister when she passed away. It was incredible because I couldn't remember much of anything else at that point, and just remembering day to day activities like brushing my teeth, driving to the store, or remembering my way home for instance was still vague, but that single memory was crystal clear. It gave me happiness, joy, and made me feel love for something in a way that I had hope for the future. It was hope that I needed badly because it was a very dark time in my life when I felt especially lonely. That memory was an anchor to reality for me and I was hanging on for dear life at that point trying to make my way back to a place where I could start to rebuild a life for myself. The memory has always been one of the most precious things in my life because it was such a phenomenal experience. In retrospect now, I realize why I kept hearing the phone ringing the night before. It's because that is how the memory begins, the day that my sister passed all began with a phone call. All I can remember is................

The Phone Call

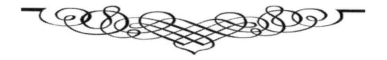

I couldn't sleep the night before, then the phone rang. "What's up?", I could hear my little sister crying in the background. "Can you meet us at P.G. Hospital because Keisha was found not breathing." The crying in the background got louder. "Mommy and Sis are not doing well, so uh, please meet us at the hospital, okay? Love ya'll!"

From that call, it was like my senses were heightened, my smell, my hearing, my vision, and my taste. It was as if I instantly began interpreting everything from a spiritual perspective. It was wild because it was like someone flipped a switch and, in that instance, God showed me exactly what was unfolding at my sister's house when they found her.

It was February 18, 2009, at 7:12 am........................

My little sister, Keisha was found face down on the floor of her bedroom, motionless and with no pulse! Her kids were going to school that morning, but they overslept waiting for their mother to wake them up like she had done every morning for ten years. They were used to that morning routine, but On February 18,2009, their world changed forever.

As they awoke by themselves, each one rubbing their eyes, they each slowly went into their mother's room, they noticed their mother's motionless body, face down on her bedroom floor. They ran quickly toward her to wake her, shaking her and shouting, "Ma! Get up, get up!!", but she wasn't moving, and they quickly realized that she didn't have a pulse and she was blue all over. They were in panic, first calling my parents, "Papa! My Mom's not breathing and she's on the floor not moving, and she doesn't have a pulse!", my Dad responded, "Call the ambulance!". Once the paramedics arrived, they tried CPR for several minutes, but they could not get a pulse. They all watched the paramedics do everything to save Keisha. A call to my other sister was later placed and she came to the house immediately. The outcome was very devastating for the entire family. At that moment, all I could think about was a conversation we had when she was 5. Keisha asked me, "Where is heaven? Can we fly there or take a bus? How does heaven look? What should I wear? Can we go see heaven one day? Can we go together one day, just us two, big brother? Can we..."

In utter disbelief, I closed my eyes and God gave me a vision of Keisha having a conversation with Him and I was able to hear her when she asked God if she could bring me with her so that we could see heaven together. God told her, "Yes, you can. Go get your big brother Quest, so you can share this experience together, so Quest can enlighten others of his journey to and from heaven." I got really scared because I'm thinking, "now wait a minute, hold up! How is that going to happen?," then I thought, "I was only kidding when we were talking about it way back..", but this is reality and we are in this moment and all I could think then was, "How are we going to get there? I mean, to go to heaven you gotta die! Hold up....", I was extremely nervous! I was stuttering so bad in my mind, that I couldn't get a word out other than, "HEAVEN?!?!?! How are we going to get to heaven?!?!?!", and I envisioned her saying, "oh, it's going to happen!," I was just really becoming paranoid, especially not knowing what or how this was all going to go down. At the same time, it made me super calm all at the same time! Remembering the conversation in my head I'm telling myself, "I'm hallucinating, yeah, I'm definitely hallucinating!"

    I sat on my sofa in utter disbelief, with a blank stare on my face really trying to convince myself that hearing Keisha talking to God was not real because it was so overwhelming to me imagining how in the world would I be able to visit heaven without dying first? I ain't going to lie, it gave me anxiety and I had never felt that kind of anxiety!

I Must Be Dreaming

As I sat on my sofa, totally numb, I called my sister Ty back, just to make sure I wasn't dreaming. Again, I was told as she answered the phone (crying uncontrollably). "Keisha wasn't breathing, Q! She wasn't breathing! She was lying on the floor when the kids found her, she was motionless. Please get here soon! Please! I love you", "Okay, I love you more," I replied. At that moment, all I could hear was my heartbeat pounding out of my chest. I couldn't hear anything else. All I know is that I felt different, really different and I could feel that something was happening to me. I walked to the bathroom and ran the water. As I lowered my hand under the faucet, all I could hear was my heartbeat getting louder and louder. As I listened to my heartbeat, I noticed my pupils were large. When I looked in the mirror, my pupils wouldn't adjust to the light at all. I could smell the water from the faucet, it smelled like rain. I could hear this buzzing noise from my living room.

There was a fly in the blinds of the window. How can all this be happening to me now? What is going on with me? I kept asking myself. I heard chimes in the air, but the ones hanging on my balcony weren't moving at all. I asked myself what was going on. As I stood there amazed and confused, I called my sister again. She answered the phone, "Where are you?". I replied, "I'm coming! How long was she not breathing?" "A very long time! Too long, Quest, too long! She's not going to make it, but we're praying." I hung up the phone and I could see what was going there at Keisha's house every time I blinked, but this was only in my mind. How am I able to see what's going on there? I kept blinking and every time I blinked; I could see a little more of what was happening over there. It felt like everything was happening in slow motion.

The next thing I saw was a vision of an EMT was bringing Keisha downstairs on a stretcher. Ty had explained in her call that there were seven of them. Four were carrying her motionless body. The other three were pumping her chest. In the background, I could hear, "Come on, Keisha," they were saying over and over again, and my Mom was crying hard. Screams filled the airwaves. I knew that she was gone. Ty also explained that her hands, lips, and feet were blue. "She's gone."

"Keisha!" "She's gone. Please hurry up and get here, please!" "I'm leaving right now. I love ya!" The details of my conversation with Ty were just playing over and over in my mind. I will never forget those two words ever again "She's gone". I started to cry, and it felt like a part of my soul left my body. I was trying to hold my tears back, but I just couldn't. I told myself to take a deep breath. As I took my deep breath, I heard someone's voice telling me to take another. This voice sounded just like my little sister's voice. Impossible! Impossible, I thought to myself! So, I told myself it wasn't her voice.

In a whispered voice I heard, "Hey, Big Brother, it's me. Are you coming to see me?" "Keisha!", this was crazy! How could I hear her voice right now?

I shouted out, "NO! No, not my baby, not Keisha, no, no, no!!!". I shouted so loud; it was as if someone was standing in my living room! I was walking toward my front door. Why am I tripping out? I thought to myself. No! I'm hallucinating! Yeah, I am! I looked around again as if Keisha was right in front of me. "Hey, Big Brother!". "Who is that?" I shouted out. I turned down the volume to the radio, I had been listening to while getting ready for my day, just to make sure I wasn't hallucinating, and before I left my house, I could hear Keisha's voice again.

This time really clear, "That's it, Big Brother."

"What do you mean, that's it?" I shouted with tears running down my face. I needed some fresh air because I felt like I was losing my mind. I tried to block what I just heard out of my mind but walking outside wasn't the same! This time, Wow! As I walked outside, all my senses were working on overload. As I walked outside, I could smell snow in the air. It wasn't supposed to snow that day. I made eye contact with this bird flying past me. She was flying in slow motion. I felt like I could hear this bird's thoughts. She was looking for a place to make a bird's nest. I could hear every flap of its wings as if this bird was trying to tell me something. She turned her head, and we connected eye to eye. Without thinking about it, I could zoom in closer and see every feather move so smoothly. I noticed the dry grass dangling from her beak. As she looked to build her nest, I could feel a connection with that one glance. That connection I felt was real because it reminded me of a time in my childhood when I used to go out on the rooftop of my house and feed the squirrels and the birds. I had a feeling that I was supposed to go back in the house, but look for her on the other side of the house because I saw her fly around the back of the house, so I went to see if she would be there and sure enough, it was like she was sitting there waiting for me. When I got to the other side of the house, I watched her for several minutes just observing her finishing her nest, intertwining the grass in a way that wove it together to make it stronger. It was amazing to me to watch her move, in fact, she allowed me to get close enough to pet her head, then she flew away. That was really special to me because it made me think of a time in my childhood when I used to get up on the roof to feed the birds and squirrels and I needed that brief distraction from the shock of just losing my sister. It was amazing that having lost my sister, God could allow me to see life in the birth of these bird eggs. Only God can do that in the moment that I needed it most. It was beautiful and it touched my heart, but it also gave me a glimpse of hope that I needed to now deal with accepting the truth of my sister's death.

It was 9:01 a.m. when I finally got in my truck and "Halo" was playing. Ironic, right? I turned off the radio, so my mind would be much clearer, but I heard it again. Then I heard, "This is it, Big Brother" in a jovial tone. I drove to the hospital thinking, "I have to do this for her." I'm not a negative person at all. I think positively all the time. My heart knew this was it. In my mind, I thought my mind was playing tricks on me. But why? I thought, why me? As I was thinking why me, my heart and soul were telling me, "I'm sorry she's gone." I started thinking about the first songs I played for her, Michael Jackson's "Never Can Say Good-Bye," and "Got to Be There." Those two songs played in my head until I arrived at the hospital. All I could think about was when my little sister was five years old. She was so adorable and had the funniest laugh. Her laugh would make me laugh.

When I finally arrived at the hospital, for some reason parking my truck was so hard to do, especially knowing that when I got out, I knew what was to come. I could smell snow in the air and again, I could still hear my little sister's voice.

Out of nowhere I heard, "It's okay, Big Brother. I'm okay. You're here now to care and protect me, like always, right? Just like when I was little." I thought, "Why can I hear this? Why?" Holding back tears, I started walking toward the hospital doors. Holding back my tears, I just wanted a happy outcome for my little sister.

"Please God! Please help my little sister. She's too young to die. She always helped people. You have to help her, God! You must! Please!"

As I entered the waiting room, I looked around. I didn't notice any of my family. I didn't see them at all, but I could hear people crying. I knew who was going to cry and who was very upset and just trying not to show it. I knew who was praying to God quietly to themselves. To hear all this was amazing to me. I was still in denial of the gifts I had been given, but I did know my spiritual maturity was reaching a level that I have never experienced before. I was scared. I found myself taking deep breaths to keep from feeling so much emotion because I didn't want to lose it. I felt like if they knew, they would all think I was crazy! So, I tried to hold back as much as I could. Everyone was talking to me, wanting me to help them, guide them somewhere or give them something, but I didn't know where or what I was supposed to give them. I looked around at everyone in the waiting room, but no one was moving their mouths. How was it that I could I hear all these people's thoughts? "Just believe," I told myself. How was I able to hear and feel their pain? I've always been able to hear and feel other people's thoughts and pain, but I just tried to tell myself not to go there, not now. I really didn't understand why I must be going through this now, but God was telling me something, He was telling me to just believe. As I entered the fourth floor, I heard what I thought were drums, and I thought, why are they playing drums in a hospital? I followed the sound and tried to find the source of it. I was drawn to a door and when I opened it, I realized that it wasn't drums, but it was the sound of my family's heartbeats.

The Waiting Room

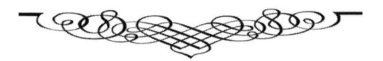

Upon entering the waiting room, around 9:13 a.m., the room was quiet and very cold. My little sister's children, my mother and father, and my other sisters were all sitting in the room nervously waiting for the doctor's. My brothers were at school and would arrive later. My nephew's grandmother (Ms. Ruth) was also with the family. Everyone in this room I loved deeply. I sat watching my sister Ty wiping my mother's tears. It was so hard to watch as every tear that came down her lovely face. It was too much to bear. One glance at my mother made me feel helpless. I'd never seen my mother cry. Never! My whole life flashed before me as I blinked. My mother had tears in her eyes when she gave birth to my little sister, Keisha. Those were tears of joy. Now she has tears of sorrow, knowing that her little girl whom she gave birth to may not be here with her anymore. I looked around the room and again and I could feel everyone's spirit. Every one of us felt helpless.

We knew that this was up to God and the medical team. I couldn't help but think about our last conversation. Keisha had asked me on Tuesday if Goofy was a dog or a walrus. We laughed so hard I could still hear her laugh. "So, God," I prayed, "I'm asking you to help my sister through this nightmare. Please God, she's young and beautiful, and she's a mother, daughter, and aunt. We need her, God! Please! My world won't be the same without her. We used to always talk about going to heaven, but this is too soon, God! Please, not now! Please, not now. Please," I begged. I was hoping for the doctors to give us some uplifting information, but there was just no way to tell. As time was ticking by so slowly, I continued to reminisce about my little sister with every tear streaming down my face. I tried to show my coolness and calmness, but it faded away the more I thought about the times we shared, it offered me a little piece of happiness that was no- where to be found in that waiting room.

    I remembered that Keisha was the first baby I had ever held. She was more than my little sister. She was my everything. I felt instant love for her. It was from her that I learned how to love, care, and share my feelings with others I loved to look at her all the time because she had the most beautiful eyes. I could see so much of myself in her, it was like she was a female version of myself, which I always thought was amazing. We shared the same mannerisms, the same humor, I was amazed at how intelligent she was, how we could have these deep conversations and she was so young! I would give her my heart if I had to. I felt so connected to her spiritually and that's what made me realize that there are many different types of love. This was a very spiritual love and I always felt like she was special because she was the first baby who I learned how to hold, the first baby I learned how to change diapers with, the first baby

I ever wiped tears for, I'd learned how to feed her, bathe her, and clothe her, and made her laugh, I mean, she was my official jokester. There was something different about the love I felt for Keisha that I keep in my heart. I would almost describe it as a bond that allowed me to feel what she felt, it came from deep within my spirit, and it was a very pure love. She was a gift from God. I taught her all of my good traits of life.

As I looked around the waiting room, I could feel and hear everyone's heartbeats speed up. Everyone's eyes looked so enlarged with sorry and emotion. I could hear my dad say to himself, "Nah, not my Keisha Weisha". He was trying to stay calm for all of us. His coolness was overtaken by his deep sadness and thoughts of memories that only he and Keisha knew about. My sister Ty was supposed to have picked her up that morning from work, so she was also very sad and taking this very hard. My parents and she were there in the apartment while Keisha transitioned. They probably already knew she was gone, but it was over whelming for us all not to just make sure that there was nothing else that could be done.

Suddenly, the door opened! Soon after, the room became colder. The doctor entered with his assistant. I could tell this wasn't going to be good. The doctor's demeanor told it all. Having been a police officer, I knew what to expect next. The doctor stood there, and I could tell it was hard for him. His tone was very dry when he spoke. There was no eye contact with our family at first. As he looked around the room at all of us, he rested his eyes on my parents. He said, "When she came in, she wasn't responding to CPR. We tried other tests. I thought that he was going to say that the tests were successful, but he said, "I'm sorry. We tried everything. She never had a pulse." The sounds of weeping soon enveloped the room, becoming louder and louder as the news sank in. I tried hard not to cry, literally doing all I could to holdback my tears. The doctor said, "Two at a time can go in to see her." My parents went first, comforting each other. I held Ty, as she cried on my chest. Every tear seemed to go through my chest, reaching my heart. My heartbeat seemed to comfort Ty. As tears eventually flooded my eyes, I couldn't help but to remember my little sister just being alive and well; laughing with me, Dad talking to my mom, I even remembered my last conversation with Keisha. She was asking me about Goofy! To hear she never had a pulse, meant she was never coming back, and all I could do was think of her children whose ages ranged from two to five years old and they represented many of her happiest moments. My mind went blank, and my just soul mourned.

Even as I was writing this, the impact of the memory still takes my breath away and fills me with so much emotion that I remember the tears literally washed away the ink the from the pages as I wrote. I had to put down my pen and gather myself… it happens every time.

Feeling Numb.......

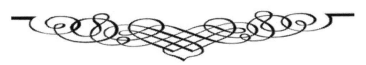

The family sat and we comforted each other, but there were no words to be spoken. All we could do is just look at each other with tears streaming down our faces. I could not fathom the loss of my little sister or any of my other sisters for that matter. I had thoughts of dying, perhaps in my old age, but I couldn't imagine someone's death when someone is twenty-nine and healthy! To think Keisha and I would never hug each other again was troublesome to me because I always imagined her just being there. Who was going to laugh at all my jokes? Every day she told me she loved me. It was a special way that she would say it and smile afterwards. I would say, "I love you, Keisha," and she would say, "Mmmmm, I love you too, Big Brother."

The look on my parents' face was unforgettable. My dad stepped out the room for a moment to catch his breath, and most times, his eyes are hazel, but when he came back into the waiting room, his eyes were lime green. The look on their faces seemed to mirror my own feelings when I was at home, first receiving the news. I have never seen my parents cry, so to see both parents crying was unbearable. It was so painful for me to watch them. My mother's face has always been a very beautiful tone, but this day her face was pale, her pupils dilated, and her hands were shaking uncontrollably. All I could do was hug my mother. I felt like her baby again. She was inconsolable. Again, I had to take a break as I wrote because even thinking about this moment is unbearable, my tears eroded the words on the page as I wrote them.

Following the tears, I remember a memory of when Keisha was three years old. It was a nice sunny day and I was lying down in the back room, resting. Out of the blue, she popped up! "Big Brother!", her clothes weren't matching at all, she had on pants with a skirt. The shirt didn't match, but she didn't care. All she wanted to do was play kickball with me. When she asked, I told her, "Not right now, I'm tired." She said, looking like a lost puppy with those big beautiful eyes, "Okay, Big Brother." I replied, after looking at her, "Okay! How could I say no, with you looking at me like that with them big ole eyes! Go in your room and get your shoes on." With the most joyful smile, she said, "Yes! Me and Big Brother are going to play!"

I instructed her how to kick the ball a couple of times; and I told her that if she did well, then we could go get some ice cream. In the front yard, she got in position. She started dancing in one spot, so happy to play with this big smile plastered on her face! I rolled the ball toward her, very slowly. She kicked the ball. It went high toward the right side, hitting the house! She was laughing so hard! I said, "Girl, what are you doing? I rolled the ball straight to you." I was laughing because she was laughing. She would do this funny dance with her shoulders, going up and down, snapping her fingers. I rolled the ball again, bop! The ball hit the same spot. She laughed again really loudly!

She said, "I'm trying, Big Brother. I'm trying!", I replied, "I know! I know! Don't tell me and show me! Girl come here! Girl, no wonder you keep kicking the ball to the right. Your shoes are on the wrong feet!" I said. We laughed so hard!

Another memory was when Keisha was four years old, she had this idea for us to bake a cake.

"Okay," I said. She knew that if we made a cake, she could lick the bowl. So, we got the cake mix out of the cabinet, we started mixing the eggs, oil, butter, and water. I leaned over and heated the oven to 350 degrees. We put the mix in the pan, and then there was a knock at the door, it was my best friend Al. When I opened the door, Al asked if I was coming out to play basketball. I told him, "No! Not right now cause I'm baking a cake with my little sister. Later I will, I promise."

I came back in the kitchen and my little sister had been eating all the cake mix! She had cake mix all over her face! I said, "This is going to be the smallest cake! You can't eat it before we bake it!" With the look of a cake bandit, she said, "We can eat it before Mommy and Daddy get home."

"Okay!" I opened the oven but noticed that it wasn't hot. "Wow!" I said. "The pilot light is not working." I reached for some matches, but I didn't know she had turned the gas on high and it was running the whole time! I lit the first match, it blew out. Then I lit the second match, but it blew out. "Keisha, we have one match left." I struck the match, and it went, WOOSH! I turned around, looked right at her, really slow. She burst into laughter, holding her stomach from laughing so hard. She said, "Go look in the mirror!"

I could feel my skin tingling and my hair smelled burnt! I felt my eyelids tightening as well. I looked in the mirror and I shouted, "Keisha, "Keisha!" She started laughing again!

My eyebrows were completely gone! Completely burned off! No eyelashes, no eyebrow, everything was just GONE! My little sister said, "I have a magic marker! I took the magic marker in the bathroom with me. I tried to work my magic to color them in, but again, not happening! Nope! So, I took off one of my socks and stretched it around my head, just like a headband. My dad came home and called me. I came out of the bath- room, but I hadn't realized he had made it home yet. I tried to keep my distance, but he asked me to come into the kitchen. He said, "What's on your head, boy?" I said, "My Kung Fu Headband!" He said, sniffing, "What's that smell?" Keisha was laughing still. I didn't realize that I was burned, and the smell was coming from me! "What smell? What's burning?", I said. I looked at my little sister with a mad look! She was whispering, "Please! Please! Don't tell on me!" I mumbled, "The oven tried to kill me!" My dad said, "WHAT?" I said, "I burned something in the oven." She never said another word about it ever again.

As I reflected on all of these wonderful memories, my tears have gone from tears of pain to tears of joy....again, the tears fade the words on the page as I continued to write.

The Blueprint

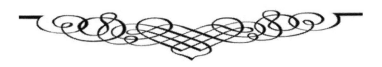

As the family mourned in the waiting room, it was time for each family member to view Keisha's body. Ms. Ruth was Keisha's children's grandmother and she was with the family in the waiting room. Ms. Ruth brought Keisha's kids with her too when she went to view the body to be their support emotionally. As she walked back into the waiting room after viewing Keisha's body, she returned to the waiting room and found everyone's faces were just life- less. It was such an unbearable sight. I didn't even want to look at them, because I knew I would lose it! I put myself in the same space as their souls in that moment and I could feel their pain at the core of my soul. My mother tried to hold back her tears. This is not just my little sister. I helped raise her, so it felt like she was my own daughter. She was my blueprint for raising a daughter. The way I cared for Keisha is the same way I care for my kids.

I could feel every beat of my heart, just working overtime, beat after beat. Soon my heartbeat began to slow down, and every blink became a flash of light. That flash of light became a polaroid of my little sister's life. I really wanted this to be a dream, but it wasn't. It was reality. I shook my head in disbelief. "This cannot be happening to us. This cannot be happening. "God, not my little sister! Not my little sister, Keisha," as the tears streamed down my face.

"This cannot be happening to us," I kept telling God over and over. Ty and I were the only ones left in the waiting room who hadn't gone in to see Keisha. I was so overwhelmed at the thought of seeing her dead made me feel like concrete was on my feet and I couldn't move. As we started walking toward Kei- sha's room to view her body, every step was a nightmare. I just couldn't catch my breath quick enough. I have noticed that my senses are heightened when I've encountered emotional experiences and I sometimes start to notice numerical patterns. When I closed my eyes, I just knew that I would reach her within fourteen steps. I was hoping this was all a dream. With seven steps to go, my eyes were still closed, I saw a white and silver shadow moving over Keisha, so I opened my eyes and let my sister Ty walk ahead of me, thinking that if Ty fainted, I would catch her instead of her having to catch me after fainting!

She's Alive

As Ty and I walked in, Keisha lie there, looking lifeless, her eyes were slightly opened. I grabbed her hand, and it was cold. I suddenly thought I heard her say something. So, I leaned in closer to listen. In a whisper, I thought I heard her say, "Take my hand, Big Brother."

"Yes, Keisha! Oh my God! You're alive! She's alive! Girl, you scared all of us! You almost didn't make it, girl."

She told me to take her hand. I noticed that one of her nails was hanging off her finger. As I held her hand, I noticed that there were some band aids sitting on a shelf next to the hospital bed, so I reached for a band-aid to wrap around her finger and while I put the band aid on, I noticed she was breathing kind of slow. Her eyes opened, just a little bit, and I heard Keisha speak! She said, "I'm ok Big Brother."

As Ty and I stood there, Ty didn't say much at all. I said, "I love you, Keisha. Girl, I love you." That's all I kept saying, kissing her forehead and holding her cold hand. I was so overwhelmed that she was talking to me.

I noticed her stomach was moving, still kind of slow. As we looked eye-to-eye, she said with a soft whisper, "Hey, Big

Brother! Hey, Big Brother. I love you so much."

I kept saying, "Let me go get Ma and Pops and the doctor! You made it back, girl! You made it back, Keisha! My little sister made it back!" Ty just looked at me. I was still crying because I couldn't believe it. I leaned down to kiss her forehead, which was slightly cold. I was shocked! I took a deep breath. After my deep breath, my hearing became amplified, just like at my house. I didn't have to lean over her now to hear her. I held her cold hand, and we connected eye-to-eye, spirit to spirit.

Keisha said, "As I lie here, one by one people are coming in and starting to weep?" Go get my family and friends! Quick! Hey family!" she called, smiling with one tear in her eye. I thought I saw everyone start walking back into the room, but now I know it was all happening in the spirit.

"How are you feeling?" we asked. "So happy that everyone's by my side," she replied, "Thanks for helping me as my soul starts to depart." I watched in complete amazement; I couldn't stop looking at her. Her face, her hair, her lovely eyes, hands, and her nails. As I stroked her hair, I remembered all the times I would comb her hair when my Mom was at work. I leaned over to give her a kiss. My lips touched her cold forehead. I said, "I love you, Little Sis, you know you'll always be my heart."

She said, "I love you too, Big Brother. I love you, too." I was in shock because she was talking, but with a breathing tube in her mouth.

Spirit to Spirit

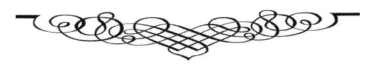

At that moment, Ty knew something wasn't right with me. I was getting upset because no one came to Keisha's aid. "Someone comes quick and take the tubing out of her mouth! It's hard for her to talk!" I yelled. All this time, Keisha hadn't come back to life. She had passed on. I was talking to her spirit, which exited through her forehead. Her spirit looked hazy. Along with the haziness, I saw sparkles. It looked like someone threw silver glitter in the air. Even her hair was sparkling. I thought I was dreaming, and I couldn't wake up. Her spirit just hovered over her body like a small cloud. At the time, I didn't know what the cloud of smoke was that was hovering over her body and forehead. At that moment, I realized that she was dead. I was still confused about what had happened when I kissed her on the forehead. I didn't know how to use my "gift" yet. Keisha was showing me how to use it unbeknownst to me. That's why my sister, was looking at me so strange. I was communicating spirit-to-spirit with Keisha I was so fascinated but puzzled. Ty couldn't communicate with Keisha's spirit like I could. I didn't want to ask her why she didn't connect the way I could because I didn't know how to ask her, so I just stood there in shock.

    I asked if she was okay. For some reason I felt happy yet sad seeing Keisha lying there dead. As Keisha lay there, I noticed her eyes were sparkling. There was one sparkling tear that wouldn't fall, as if to say, "Good-bye, Big Brother, and thank you so much for listening to me. Thank you for showing me what love is and everything about life. I'll miss you and I love you so much. Thank you, Ty, for always being there for me and my big brother. I have admired you my whole life. I wanted to be just like you Big Brother." I just couldn't let Keisha's hand go. Love wouldn't let me let it go.

    My heart was crying so much. My deep voice became so soft, like a butterfly flapping its wings. Still in shock and confused, I wished I could keep her last tear from falling. Ty kept saying, "Let's go now Quest. I'm here for you now."

    As I let my little sister's hand go, I placed them gently on her stomach. That last tear slowly ran down her cold face, sparkling like a diamond. I felt a breeze pass by me. I knew it was Keisha. I glanced back one more time before exiting her room. Again, I told her I loved her so much. I felt the tears streaming down my face uncontrollably now. I could hear her soft voice, "I love you, too, Big Brother. I'm okay. I'm okay." Her eyes closed as we walked away. I kept saying, "I love her so much. I love her so much," as Ty and I walked out of Keisha's room, holding hands, I asked her, "What am I going to do now? I'll never be the same again."

    I sat next to my parents. I closed my eyes, tears streaming down my face, thinking, Why God? Why my little sister?

I remember caring for her as a young girl. She always wanted to share everything. I remember all the things were shared together, like her first birthday; riding her bicycle; playing kickball; playing jacks; cards; picking flowers so she could put them in her hair; showing her how to dress; putting on makeup; being a young lady; answering her questions about boys and growing up. When she graduated from high school, she was ready for the world. At least she thought she was! Her wonderful life cut short. I still don't understand. I still miss talking and laughing with her.

Is There A Heaven?

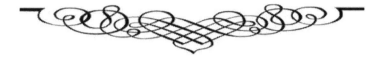

I remember a time when my mother was working. She would call home and tell me to go get my little sister from day care. The distance seemed very far, but knowing when I picked her up she would be so happy to see me, I didn't really care about the long walk. Every time I picked her up, she would come running. "Big Brother! Big Brother!" When she came out, she wanted to show me what she had done all day. She would ask me a thousand questions. She was very smart for her age. She would ask me, looking up at the sky, "Big Brother, is there a heaven up there?" I would look up at the sky too.

"There sure is a heaven," I responded. "Yeah, but all those clouds in the sky! Where is heaven? Where's God? Where's Jesus? How do we get there? Can we go? You wanna go too? Do we take a bus or an airplane? What do I wear? Can you take me there?"

"Keisha! Keisha! Slow down," I said. "One day you'll be there."

Her Smile

Leaving my family at that moment was very hard for me, but I had to pick up my younger brother from school. On the way to his school, I remembered that Keisha was on the Pom-Pom Squad in 1998. I attended several of her competitions. She was so happy to be a part of the team. I enjoyed watching my little sister dance and do her thing. On the stage, she would blossom. Her smile made me happy.

Other students loved to be around Keisha. She had the most caring heart. Those who met her in person would be greeted with the warmest and most beautiful smile. I always told her, "A loving smile goes straight to the heart." Hers definitely did.

Before I got into my truck to pick up my younger brother, my spiritual consciousness was at a high level. As I looked around, my vision was again so acute. It amazed me.

It started to snow. One thing about the spiritual life, your way of life is altered forever. You don't see your surroundings the same way. Never! You can be afraid like I was at first, but you really won't see beyond your natural sight. If you trust God, the fear goes away and he can show you marvelous things!

As the snow fell, I could zoom in and out, looking at every

drop. I could see the crystals in the snow. In the spirit realm everything's three-dimensional. The snow was that clear to me. Have you ever heard snow hitting the ground? Of course not! Your ears aren't that sensitive. In the spiritual realm, you can. I could hear snow falling, touching the ground ever so softly. My dad could see the snow falling as well. He would tell later me in the day about it. Looking around, people and cars were passing me. I could see the moles on their faces, if they had any. I noticed the sadness in people's eyes very quickly. I also keened in on scratches and dings on trucks and cars that passed me by.

At the moment that I walked out of the hospital looked straight up in the sky. Yes, the snow was falling and gently touching my face. What I saw next really fascinated me. I saw water drops that transformed into snow right before my very eyes. I didn't blink the whole time I was looking up.

At that time my soul and my spirit asked God, "Why must you take my sister now? Why?

She's twenty-nine years old. All she talked about was turning thirty." God answered me, "Quest, I need her here now, my son." I didn't attend church like I normally would, however, after this experience, I planned on attending church on a regular basis so that I could learn more about the connection I had with God.

First I thought someone was playing a joke on me because the voice was so mild, deep and soothing, not like my own. My voice is very deep, but it wasn't anything like the voice that I heard in my head, so I knew it wasn't me. I stood there in sheer disbelief that God was talking to me.

I couldn't help but think about one thing: "Why, out of the blue, was my little sister gone?" I started crying as I asked God several times, "Why? Why? Why?" I screamed so loud, yet nothing came out of my mouth!

To Keisha

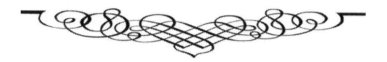

I can't help but to cry because this happened just clear out of the blue. But why me?

God has called you, so it's okay with me. The love we shared set my spirit free. My love for you, Keisha is so deep and spiritual. We're always connected.

You left without saying good-bye. I still have your text in my phone, thanking me for a being such a wonderful person in your life. I knew one day you would make someone happy to be their wife.

I'm here thinking of you. Why were you taken away? Couldn't God just wait one more day? I can still see your smile. Hear your voice saying, "I love you too." I cry so much from the thought of missing you.

I think back when you were five years old, the fresh picked flowers in your hair. I'd taught you how to share and care. Without you, my heart I can't bear.

If God gave me one more day with you, I would show the world how much I love you so, I'd tell you more and more jokes so you could laugh out loud. You're the first baby I've ever held, so now when I look up in the clouds, I'll see your beautiful face, there smiling so proudly.

Mad At God

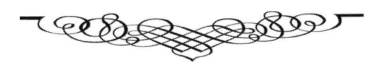

Driving home was a disaster. I thought I would never reach my destination. I wanted to yell some more! I was mad at God for taking my little sister away from me, our family and friends. I didn't want to accept the loss of her life. I told Him, "God, you could have taken a bird, dog or cat, but not my little sister!". I had stopped going to church long ago, so I thought that maybe God was punishing me. I felt that I hadn't used the gifts He gave me wisely, I never took time to learn about them, but I wanted to see if Keisha made it to heaven. I stood there in hopes that something would come to me, that maybe He would reveal to me why He chose to take her, now, but nothing happened. My vision was normal, along with my hearing and smell. Nothing!

"Thank you, God! Thank you for the gift. Was it a gift?" I thought that this was my imagination playing tricks on me. That's what I told myself. I'm probably still in shock. Yeah, I'm in shock. It didn't happen, besides, who's going to believe me anyway? No one, they'll just think I'm crazy!

I sat on my sofa, hoping this was all a bad dream. So I called my mother's house and spoke to my dad, hopefully to regain some clarity. He said, "When I came out of the hospital, I noticed the snow falling in slow motion." Hearing him say this, I didn't respond. I thought, "There's no way he saw what I saw and my mother, brothers, and sisters didn't either." I was so amazed about this revelation because I was living through the same spiritual consciousness myself! He asked me how I was doing. I replied, "I'm still in shock, Pops." He responded, "I just spoke to Keisha last night. She just came over to the house and was laughing and dancing. She was very happy. Man, I can't believe this, I just can't!" What I did notice and felt from my dad, was love. Especially the love he had for Keisha. Keisha and my dad shared a very close bond. I found out later that Dad had this secret that he never really talked about at all. He was an all-star basketball player. He didn't speak of it because he didn't want anyone thinking he wasn't cool, so he didn't tell anyone about his gift for twenty-five years. All his peers thought he was one of the coolest guys. It was a huge shock when I found out that he too shared this gift, but I knew in my heart and deep in my spirit that he was telling the truth. This was his secret for all these years. My dad was spiritually gifted. He was also very creative. My dad taught us how to use our creative eye, showing us that we can see things from our surroundings that people couldn't see or fathom. We all could just stare at something, like a tree, ring, leaf—anything. We all saw the same thing, however Keisha could see things very fast. She would tell my dad things even he couldn't see.

 We all could stare at a stain and try to see which one would come up with a face or picture first. Sometimes it would be me,

Ty, or Keisha. As we said our goodbyes over the phone, I tried to relax and just calm down. I heard a voice, "Just take some deep breaths and just relax. Relax, Big Brother."

My Little Sister Talking

I shouted, "Keisha, is that you?" No response. I knew it was a girl's voice. I couldn't relax after what I had heard.

That night it was hard for me to go to sleep. I called my girlfriend over to watch me sleep. She couldn't make it because she had kids of her own to look after. That night I didn't go to sleep. I couldn't sleep. My mind was overwhelmed. I couldn't begin to try to think straight! As I drifted off, I felt I was being watched. I started to hear real quiet voices. My mind must be playing tricks on me again, I thought. I still hadn't no sleep for two days!

On Friday, I asked my girlfriend again to come watch me sleep. This night I was exhausted. I thanked her for coming to watch over me that night. I sat on the end of my bed. I almost started crying, but I held myself together as best as I could. I started thinking about my little sis, how she was doing. Was she okay? Was she safe? I said, "Keisha, give me a sign that you're okay." A minute passed, and there was no sign. Then it happened.

My air vent was completely closed. It just opened up by itself. My girlfriend said, "Okay, tell me your air vent didn't just open by itself!" I said, "You're not going to believe me, but that was my little sister telling me she's okay."

I wanted to tell her everything that happened to me. Then I thought, she wouldn't believe me anyway. Some people can't fathom what I had experienced or heard. I started having spiritual dreams, but these dreams were not like other dreams that I had experienced in the past. They were vivid and filled with brilliant colors. All I kept hearing in my dreams were voices: male and female. Voices telling me to believe in my spiritual connections and have faith. I awoke to voices, chimes, my little sister laughing, people clapping, cheers, music, and then it happened. I was in my bedroom when I heard my sister's voice, "Big Brother!" I got up thinking my sons had left the patio doors open.

As I walked toward the patio doors, I reached for something to protect myself, thinking someone had broken into my house. I heard several men's voices coming from somewhere in my home. I had a home alarm, but it didn't alert me. But all the voices and noises did. It was like they were partying out on my patio! I stepped closer but noticed the voices and sounds drifting away from the patio. I went outside to check the surroundings but found nothing suspicious. I re-entered my house, making sure I locked everything. I returned to my bedroom, not thinking anything of it. I put my hands behind my head. "Hey, Big Brother!" It was my little sister's voice. I thought I was dreaming, but her voice sounded so clear through all of that cheering. I shouted, "Keisha! Is that you? Keisha! Keisha!"

As I ran to my patio again, I noticed my chimes on the patio weren't moving, but I could hear them. The wind wasn't blowing at all. The voice didn't drift this time. I could hear them loud and clear. I just couldn't make out my sister's voice clearly because her voice was so faint. I sat down at my table near my living room and patio, just in case I heard it again.

I asked my little sister to come to me. Help me. Help me, finish her second book. The first one, Who I Am, was already a hit. At this time, as I was sitting there calmly and ready for her, I heard voices and music again. This time I wasn't moving. I turned, looking over my shoulder.

I heard Keisha's voice say, "Hey, Big Brother!". I was completely in shock and replied, "Keisha, is that you?", "Yeah! It's me, Big Brother!" I turned back around because now my heart was beating so fast. My law enforcement training prepared me not to be afraid, but to be calm. Yet this was different. I said, "I can't really hear you, Keisha. You're not that clear."

Within three seconds, I heard a sound like air coming out of a balloon. "Hey, Big Brother! How's that?" she asked in a crystal-clear voice.

I jumped up, gasping for air! I burst into tears and started crying. With my hands covering my face, I could hear her voice, perfectly clear. My emotions got the best of me though. I ran to my room because I was so scared! Keisha said, "Big Brother, please calm down", I said, "This can't be real. This can't be real," "Oh, my God! I can't believe this!"

Keisha said, "Oh, don't say 'can't' You have to take a couple of deep breaths for me. I know this is shocking to you, but this is real! You can see me if you calm down and take a deep breath. Just Believe! Believe! All you have to do is believe that you can see me and you will. You see, God sent me for you. We want to show you heaven."

I said, "God sent you? Did I die? Am I dead?". I started crying harder, almost having a panic attack. "Why did you leave me? Why, Keisha? Why? You were so young. How can I live without you?". Keisha replied, "It's okay, Big Brother." "No, it's not! "I love you so much, Keisha. I Love you!" I said hysterically. Keisha replied, "Listen, I need you to calm down, right now!". Suddenly, my tears slowed as I began to calm down. "That's it, Big Brother. You don't have to cry anymore. I'm okay." Keisha said. As my emotions settled, I started to see radiant stars. I opened my eyes again, unsure of what I had just seen. Wow! My little sister's whole body was covered in beautiful stars—green, purple, white, silver, yellow, and gold. Her face was golden. I started to calm down but was still in shock. As she reached out to touch me, I jumped back. Was it going to hurt if she touched me? Her hands began to touch my face, ever so softly. "It's okay, Big Brother. I'm not here to hurt you. Remember that time when I was five and we were walking home from school talking about going to heaven? And you were telling me what you thought heaven looked like?". As I started to remember, I replied, "Yeah." Then, I started crying so loudly that I thought I might wake up my sons.

The memory took me straight back to that moment and it just hurt so bad to relive that moment with her knowing that she is really gone now. It was truly remarkable. She said, "I remember when we were walking home from school that day and we stopped and looked up through the trees and there were those beautiful clouds? You told me that is where heaven was. I asked you if we could take a bus or an airplane to go visit there one day, and you told me that you could only go there if you died. I remember I started crying because I didn't want you to die! You told me that you weren't going to die, that you were going to live a long time, and I asked you if we could go there together and you said, we sure can, one day". At that moment, I just couldn't stop shaking and crying. Keisha said, "Well, today is that day Big Brother, today is the day we are going to heaven together." I was completely in shock! I got chills because I was thinking about the reality of it wondering, how are we going to get there? So I asked her, "How? Do we have to die? Did I die? Hold up………ok, now wait, how are we going to do this? Keisha started laughing and said, "Big Brother, calm down! Just believe." I replied, "I just can't help it, Keisha. I don't want you to go. Please don't go, Keisha," I pleaded and she said, "but I'm already gone, Big Brother." When she said that it just hit like a ton of bricks! It hurt SO BAD and the reality check was harsh.

Even though I was crying, I opened my eyes to see if my sons were awake. Tears were just streaming down my face. Keisha said, "They're not going to wake up until we are done. God has things under control. He really wants you to see heaven. He wants you to be the one who will tell people what you saw. They need to know that heaven is real."

I was beyond shocked and I asked her, "How will I remember everything?", Keisha replied,

"You will! You have a gift that God gave you. You just haven't believed in the gift or yourself all this time. The angels are waiting to guide you around heaven too." I said, "Angels? Real angels? Why me?" Keisha said, "Yeah! Go over to the wall where the poster frames are resting.", and I was thinking to myself, "Hold up, you can see that!?!? How did you know I had picture frames against my wall?" Keisha said, "Yeah, I see everything through your eyes." Every blink I took, I could see my little sister's face and body so clearly. I was still very afraid, and she knew it, telling me to calm down and believe. "Why me, Keisha, of all people? Why is God trusting me?". "Because, God made you special. All these years you've been in denial about your spiritual gifts. So now, today, you're going to connect with the angels, so, just relax, it'll be okay. Just think, Big Brother, all this time you didn't know you had a gift? But I knew you did".

"How can I relax when you're talking about angels and going to heaven? Plus, I'm talking to a ghost!". "But, I'm not a ghost," she said, laughing. I started laughing myself because she was laughing. "I'm not here to haunt you, dummy! I want to show you where I'm at. Now look through your picture frame."

I looked through each frame stopping at each one to ask her if that was one she was talking about. "Not that one. Not that one! No, not that one! Nope! Nope! Yes! Yes! This one! This is where I am now, in paradise", Keisha was pointing to the picture that looked like paradise. I said, "Right now? But you're here with me!?!?". I didn't get it. Then, Keisha said, "I can travel at the speed of light.", and I was like, "Yeah, right, Keisha!". Keisha said, "Really, (giggling) if you believe! I can take you.

Do you believe?". I said, "Yeah, I believe. I'm talking to you, so I believe!", she responded, "Do you really? Ok, turn the picture sideways." "How did you know the picture was sideways?" and she reminded me, "Because I'm looking through your eyes." I said, "My eyes?". "Yeah. I can see things differently in the eyes of the spirit. It's kind of like seeing things in 3D. We share that trait, remember? I always knew you could, that's why I was calling you, because I knew you had the ability to hear and see me." I always knew there was something special about how I could see things, I just couldn't explain it. I said, "Yeah! How did you know that?", she replied, "Because I've always had the spiritual awareness and I can be anywhere in the world at any time now. You can see things in a way that other people can't see. Like me talking to you at the hospital. Ty blocked me out, but you could hear and communicate with me. That's probably why you felt a breeze, huh? That was me passing through you."

"I thought I was imagining that when I was talking to you. I thought I was dreaming."

"No! That was real. But afterwards, you didn't believe it was me. So, I floated around for a while, until you were more focused. I was flying around until your spirit opened up, the deep breaths you were taking really helped you get focused." I said.

"Hold up, hold up, hold up……So wait, it was you who opened my air vent?". "Yeah, that was me! Did I scare you?" "Uh Yeah! Because I have to close that vent with two fingers because the arm is broke."

"Can you teach me what I need to learn about my gifts?", "I sure can. That's why I'm here with you right now, Big Brother and the angels will teach you too."

"Really? Okay, I'm sorry. What's up with this picture of paradise?" "That's where I'm at now." The picture showed several palm trees, white sand, crystal clear ocean water, lovely clouds, and two doves flying in the air. Paradise!

"Look carefully. Look, I'm in the middle; that dot." "Oh, I see it!" "That's another dove. The dot is the dove's eyes." "I never noticed it before because it blends in with the clouds." "Right, it does. But, that's me! The other two are you and Ty. Sit down for this one. Watch the dove. Believe in yourself, take a deep breath………..Now four more deep breaths."

Paradise

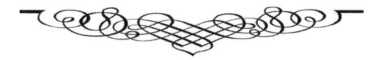

Suddenly I could feel the spiritual realm opening. I felt my senses heightening because as I glanced over, I could smell the soil in my pot- ted plant. For every deep breath I took, I could feel a breeze flowing through my shirt.

Keisha said, "Open your spiritual eyes and believe, Big Brother." As I looked at my little sister, she looked normal just covered in a mist of stars. I felt my spiritual eyes opening, my body felt weightless. I stood up and moved toward Keisha, we both just started laughing, just like when she was five years old again. I asked her, "Why are you laughing?", she said, "Look behind you!" I turned slowly to look behind me and I saw myself.

Quest: "Wow! He looks like me!"

Keisha: She said, "That's you, crying at the table."

Quest: "But, if that's me, how can I be with you?" I asked."

Keisha: "You're having an out-of-body experience. Your spirit is free."

Quest: "Wow! Can I fly?" I asked.

Keisha: "You can fly and do other amazing things."

As I looked back at myself I saw myself sitting at the table with my eyes closed, tears were flowing down my face.

"Now, look at the dove." The dove in the picture's wings started flapping. I looked at my physical self with bewilderment and concern, but I remained calm. As I watched myself at the table, my physical body, I watched my tears subside and my physical body began to calm.

I watched my physical body again I saw my eyes opening again. In that moment, I realized that I was moving between my physical and my spiritual self. Keisha said, "Now close your eyes,"

Quest: "How am I going to explain this to anyone? They're gonna think I'm crazy!"

I felt myself slipping deeper into the spiritual realm, I watched myself still sitting at the table, but with my eyes closed and my arms down by my sides.

Quest: "How can I see myself? Did I die?"

Keisha: "No! This is how you get to heaven. We are doves."

In that moment, I really felt weightless. I really couldn't see anything as I looked deeper into the picture, except this brilliant light. I started to notice a sparkling mist around the doves in the picture and as I went to mention it to Keisha, I turned and looked at her and saw the mist all around her and within seconds, I started to see the mist all around me. That's when I started to feel even more weightless. I looked back again and saw myself at the table and it was just so incredible to see myself. It was shocking at first, but so blissful at the same time. I could see my every move.

Quest: "People are going to think I'm crazy, Keisha!"

Keisha: "No they're not! It's okay, Big Brother." Then,

just like that, she began elevating then she passed right through the ceiling. I just stood there in disbelief! I took another look at myself at the table. Then I heard Keisha saying, "Come on, Big Brother!". She coaxed me to join her, but that would mean I had to pass through the ceiling. Then, Keisha's voice got started to get faint as she said, "Believe! Just believe!"

I looked up at the ceiling and noticed it was getting closer to me. I felt my faith growing because I didn't want to miss this moment with her, so I started to believe and I opened my eyes just before my head touched the ceiling. Then, whoosh! I had passed right through the ceiling and started floating through the sky.

Keisha yelled, "Come on, you can do it, Big Brother!". So, I closed my eyes again, spread my arms out, and started rising into the sky. As I opened my eyes, all I saw was white light, then a brilliant wave of colors that weren't familiar to me.

"Follow my voice…..". As I flew toward her voice, I was really enjoying all the colors, and then everything suddenly turned white again! As we ascended, I saw a vivid white light, then a baby blue and then, I finally caught up with her. "Wow! That was incredible! Are we in heaven?"

We started flying towards a bright, crystal-like light. I could feel my spirit being pulled toward the light. I felt this loving feeling drawing me closer. Then, I looked over and I saw my sister Ty flying through the clouds, so I followed her. Keisha came flying through the clouds last. As we continued our journey, it was like we passed through various sections progressively as we headed into heaven. The things I saw were phenomenal. As we were flying, I felt more alive than I ever have. I saw the most beautiful palm trees that were just swaying in the breeze; you could smell tropical fruit like coconuts, bananas, and pineapples in the air. I said, "This place must be heaven, Keisha!" Keisha giggled and said, "We are in paradise!".

I was confused when she said that, so I said, "So wait, this isn't heaven?" and Keisha replied, "Nope. This is where you come to fly and be with your loved ones. This is the place where the three of us can enjoy all of our memories together, and to love on each other one last time before I go to heaven."

I asked Keisha, "Why us and not Mom and Dad?", and Kei- sha replied, "God told me to come get you." Then I said, "Yeah, but Ty is here, too." Keisha replied, "As your belief started to grow more and more, you called her here through your belief and didn't even know it". I said, "I did?" I asked her, "Can Ty hear me? Are we doves? How are we doves?" Keisha said, "Just enjoy the moment, silly! Ty can hear you, not me." I asked, "Why not? Keisha replied, "Your spirit is connected to me in a special way".

All three of us are flying over the crystal, clear sparkling, water. I could feel the sunbeams on my wings and the smell of fruit in the air. So breathtaking to look down and see tropical fish or dancing dolphins swimming with your shadows. I felt this energy of love from them. Even the waves had a connection with us. "I love it, Keisha! It's so beautiful!"

"And I love you, Big Brother!"

We continued to fly through the beautiful palm trees with the smell of fruit in the air. I looked over at both sisters as they continued to fly in harmony, wings flapping as one. It was wonderful, in flight, enjoying God's kingdom. The look on Ty's face was blissful. Nothing more perfect. Nothing like watching my sisters flying together. At that moment, Keisha told me, "When the spirit leaves the body of someone who has passed over to the other side, it hovers over them for a while. Keisha said, "I could see myself lying there. I didn't know that I had passed away. It happened so suddenly. I hadn't even said hello, good-bye, or I love you yet to anyone that day. I'm still in shock, but glad to have my brother and sister to share this journey with me. When my spirit left the hospital, I came outside with all of you." Ty was in awe and speechless as we both listened to Keisha tell us how this all works.

Keisha went on to tell us, "As everyone stood there in the waiting room talking, I didn't know who to ride with! But I realized I can go with everyone! This is all new to me. I can be here and there at the blink of an eye. When I was walking in the physical, I was also sitting in the van with Mom and Dad on the way to their house. I went back to their house and started thinking about all the good and bad memories I had in that house. I came to you, because we talked about heaven so many times when I was a child. Now, we're here flying over paradise together, I asked God if I could bring you because you tried to tell me what heaven looked like when God would show you in your dreams. God said, "Keisha, go get Quest. He's special, and I don't think he knows the depth of his spiritual ability," and now here you are right here with me!".

Keisha flew higher than Ty and me, she started doing figure eights in the sky and it was beautiful to watch her flying so free. No pain. No worries.

Tricks In The Air

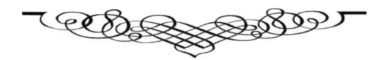

Keisha looked so peaceful, she had such a gorgeous smile on her face. I couldn't help but smile at her. With her, it felt like she was five again. She was having so much fun and seemed so free! I tried to do figure eights, but I wasn't as comfortable with my wings and felt unable to do tricks in the air. Keisha laughed at me because she knew that it was all about belief and I know she told me that, it's just that I felt so ill-equipped in the moment, but she was kind of teasing me. That's when I told her it wasn't funny, and told her that if she wasn't careful, she could break her wings! She continued doing tricks in the air that Ty and I couldn't do. Ty was flying normally, nothing fancy or creative. I wanted to enjoy everything with my sisters. So, I tried to do the figure eights again, but I almost fell out of the sky! Keisha laughed at us a lot, but as I kept falling, Keisha finally just yelled, "Believe!" and she was right, as my belief grew, I started flying normally again, flapping my wings without a thought, which I realized were really heavy, especially when I was trying to catch up to my sisters. I finally did catch up to them. My little sister said with a giggle, "Next time listen to me, Big Brother!"

As we flew through the palm trees, the air was pure, but still smelled like tropical fruit. The island sand looked soft like sugar, only it sparkled. Over the palm trees, we all flapped our wings in unison, back and forth, then up and down. It was amazing how everything in the spiritual realm seems like a symphony, as if God orchestrates it so perfectly, it can't happen that way in the natural. It was literally the love we had for each other that put us so in sync.

Keisha shouted, "Big Brother," I replied, "Yeah?" I couldn't hear her really well because the breeze beneath me was so heavenly lifting me up higher and higher every time I flapped my wings. "Hey! You, wanna see something amazing?" I answered, "This is amazing!", while enjoying flying through the soft angelic clouds Keisha said, "Look! Down!", I replied, "No way!", I asked her, "Am I seeing what I think I'm seeing?" Keisha replied, "Yes, yes you are," as she smiled so sweetly. As we flew above the crystal clear water, not only were there dolphins dancing with us, but they were dancing with our reflections.

Ty's reflection showed her wearing a brilliant dress. It sparkled as if it were alive. Diamonds trimmed the dress and sparkled off the water like shimmers as she flew over! As I looked down, I could see in my reflection and I was wearing a white suit with diamond buttons, accented with a tie that was made of diamonds, and it was so beautiful to watch as I flew by. We were fly and flying and it was amazing!

Angel Clouds

As we were flying higher and doing more tricks in the air, Keisha was guiding us through the celestial skies. Beautiful doesn't even begin to describe this place enough or the feeling you experience from being here! By now, we all had flown through so many clouds. Wow! Look at that! We were flying through clouds that looked like angels!

I asked Keisha and Ty, "Hey, you smell that?" I've smelled that same smell before. I thought it was just me, but it wasn't. "We're flying in the angel shaped clouds and they smelled like sugar cookies," Keisha said, "Yes, just like sugar cookies! We're very close." I asked, "Close to what?" Keisha said, "Heaven." I became so nervous, to the point that saw some of my feathers started falling out. Keisha said, "Stay calm! It's okay Big Brother, just stay calm!". I started freaking out and even more feathers came out! "How high are we?", Keisha said, "Very high." I tried to keep up and keep my cool, but I started to tire out all of a sudden. I flapped and I flapped my wings, I flapped again and again really hard. I was getting exhausted. Then again, Keisha seemed to share her strength with us and we began flying as one again. Ty wasn't flying at this height. She continued to fly at a lower height under the angel clouds, but I could still see her just enjoying the heavenly breezes and breathing in the sugar cookie smell. Keisha closed her wings and put her head down and then began to fly straight down like a plane, nose diving, then she shot straight up like a rocket, flying right past me! Wow! Now that's a trick! But, I noticed there wasn't a reflection of her over the water. "Hey Keisha!" I yelled. "Yeah, Big Brother?" "Okay, where's your reflection on the water?", Keisha replied, "That's what I've been trying to tell you! I don't have one!", I responded, "Yeah right! What trick is that? That's amazing, girl! How do you do that?". Keisha explained, "No! You have one because it's not your time, but I don't have one because it's almost time for me to go into heaven."

    This time I could not keep up with her. "Wait up, Keisha!" Keisha said, "God is calling me now. I have to go meet my angels." I asked, "Angels or God?" Keisha simply said, "I love you, don't worry, I'll see you again" she flew to Ty and said something to her, but I didn't get to hear what she said to Ty. I asked her as I got an inch from her wings again, "What do you mean you'll see me soon?".

    This time she looked over at me. "I love you, Big Brother." I replied, "I love you, too," and as I flapped my wings harder to try and keep up with her, I just couldn't go that high." Keisha shouted, "Big Brother, you can't fly this high. It's not your time.

    I love you!" she said as she smiled at me. "I love you. Tell Mom and Dad I love them from the bottom of my heart and that I'll see them one day again in heaven." I flapped my wings as hard and as fast as I could trying to catch up with her, but I could only get as close as our wings barely touching!". I yelled, "Keisha, wait, I" Keisha instructed me, "Big Brother, take a deep breath! Close your eyes! Now open them,". She was gone! All I saw was white clouds! I felt my eyes as they started to get heavy with tears. I felt so left behind. So alone and so sad. I could see Ty still flying around the under angel shaped clouds, so peacefully, just enjoying the fresh air under her wings. Then I heard my little sister's voice. As Keisha ascended, she turned around, looked at me and said, "Don't stop believing!"

Welcome Back

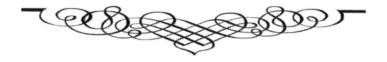

In the distance, I saw something shimmering. I asked Keisha if she saw the shimmering light and I asked her what she thought it was, but she didn't answer me. We just kept walking toward the shining object, and as we got closer, this object became larger and it became obvious that it was a very large book. My instincts told me that this was the book of life. As I looked at my sister in surprise as if I knew what it was, we just stood there smiling at each other.

We started smelling cookies again. As we looked around, no one was there. I looked back at her and asked, "What's this? Where are we?"

It seemed that in an instance, right as she said that to me, my senses were overwhelmed and super sensitive. I could see everything as if it were three dimensional.

To see yourself and everything around you in that way, it's just unbelievable! It was like I could see everything with the eyes of the spirit and it enabled me to see beyond the physical vision that your eyes normally have. I can see in all directions at once. I've had an out-of-body experience before, but this time I didn't recognize myself this time. I was still in shock that Keisha was just gone, and I felt like I was beginning to descend, then I heard God's voice call me to come back up, and before you know it, I stood right beside my little sister. I grabbed her and couldn't stop hugging her.

We started walking through the clouds and it felt like we were walking and floating at the same time. I felt weightless. In the distance, I saw something shimmering. I asked Keisha if she saw the shimmering light and I asked her what she thought it was, but she didn't answer me. We just kept walking toward the shining object, and as we got closer, this object became larger and it became obvious that it was a very large book. My instincts told me that this was the book of life. As I looked at my sister in surprise as if I knew what it was, we just stood there smiling at each other.

We started smelling cookies again. As we looked around, no one was there. I looked back at her and asked, "What's this? Where are we?"

We Enter Heaven

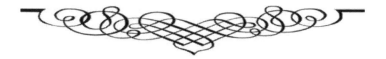

The object began to vibrate and was floating in midair. Floating! The smell of cookies became really strong. We didn't know what to think about where the smell was coming from or about this book floating. The thought tickled us, so we started laughing, because we didn't know what this was. As I stepped forward to touch it, the book moved backwards. My little sister, laughing, stepped forward, then took another step, but when she went to touch the book, it didn't move. She touched the screen and it turned on.

"This has to be the Book of Life," I said, with a serious face, "What do you mean it's the Book of Life? There is no way that it's that big, Keisha!" Keisha opened her hand, fingers stretched out and she placed them on the page. Then the pages came to life and lit up right before my eyes!

"What? How could it? No way, Keisha, no way! I've never seen a book this large before." That's all I think over and over in my head. My senses were heightened at that moment even more than before. I started hearing a baby cry. I kept saying, "I recognize that cry. I've heard it before." Keisha told me, "Of course you have; that's me!". I said, "What do you mean it's you?" The book started flashing so rapidly that physical eyes wouldn't be able to catch every flash. There was a flash of my little sister as a baby, and then flashes of all her life moments, from the time she was born right up to her passing. It was astounding!

As I stood there with her, we started laughing. It made us happy to see the first time I fed her, changed her, bathed her, and brushed her hair. They were such great memories. As the flashes slowed down, we glanced at each other, and I grabbed her hand and held it tightly, and at the same time we said, "The Book of life!"

To see my little sister at age two, then five years old just made me so emotional I wanted to cry. I could feel my eyes swelling with tears. I was so amazed and in awe of the Book of Life.

I felt breathless for several minutes, looking at every moment of her life. Just lovely!

We started smelling sugar cookies. The smell at first was very faint. The smell was like caramelizing cookies. Physically the clouds look plain and simple and the clouds just move slowly by, but these clouds literally looked like they were "dancing". We saw the clouds change colors, from white to silver, silver to purple, then purple to a brilliant yellow. All the clouds sparkled, and you could feel that the colors represented emotion, like joy. As the smell became stronger, we saw another cloud that danced right in front of us. Now I know this is going to sound pretty incredible, but as we watched the clouds trans- form, and we started to see them take shape. It looked like some- one was walking towards us, but we couldn't make out a face, or even a body. We only saw what looked like the image of the most comfortable, silky, shimmering sleep attire I've ever seen. It was the oddest thing to watch. As the figure approached us, another pair of pants came into view. Then it happened! The clouds faded away. Two people appeared; one male and one female.

The clouds seemed to hover around them, circling their chest and waist area. It looked like their skin didn't have color, almost as if they were made of pure light, only translucent. These beings had faces that were platinum and blurry, as if they were made out of stars! They walked toward us, and not knowing what to expect, I stood in front of Keisha because my instincts were to protect her. As they walked closer toward us, their faces became clearer, but I noticed the male's face first. They both looked very androgynous, different, yet beautiful. As they got closer, they became larger and larger, until they were standing in front of us as giants! Magnificent and glorious. They were so beautiful as they stood there staring at us. I was in utter awe!

They had these beautiful wings that fluttered behind them and then, they suddenly just stretched out their wings to their full length and capacity and it took us completely by surprise! I had never seen or even imagined anything like this. It was indescribable! I thought my little sister's wings were a nice size, but their wings were incredible! They started to glow, from their faces down to their perfect hands. I had to take a deep breath!

They were right in front of us, smelling like sugar cookies. I looked down at my feet. I don't know why I did that, but I couldn't see myself. I saw my little sister's feet. I was so lost.

Lost in my spirit, from the shock of it all. My sister said, "No! No you're not lost! You started crying in the physical, but it's really okay if you just stay calm in the spirit Big Brother." My mind and heart were in shock. Keisha demanded that I stop crying and just breathe, but it was difficult because I could still see myself in the physical sitting at the table crying in my house. I was in shock and so amazed. How could I see myself, so many miles away, and how was it happening so quickly? In the blink of an eye! Amazing, but true! Maybe this was Heaven's speed!

I finally stopped crying and began to focus and gain control of my breathing. My mind began focusing on being in the spiritual again so that I could enjoy this heavenly experience. My body was like a shell. My eyes were opened, but it's like I'm in a trance. I felt myself transitioning back to heaven, standing next to my little sister, as if I had never left.

I gave a sigh of relief and I couldn't help but ask them questions. I said, "Maybe it's me, but y'all smell like sugar cookies, some really good sugar cookies! You're making me hungry!" My little sister started to laugh, shaking her head! The angels turned and looked at me and started laughing! I said, "Wow, angels laugh?!?" They spoke in unison, "We sure do!" I could feel love emanating from them like a vibration. I could not ex- plain the feeling, but it felt so good! I kept getting butterflies in my stomach. For every step the angels took toward us, I became more overwhelmed with intense feelings of love, all of my thoughts were positive. I wanted to love everyone. I felt my love for people deepened immediately. I wanted to give my love to everyone. As I kept looking into their eyes, my heart was pumping love all throughout my body. The wind started to blow, and I noticed their wings were still picture-perfect! Their wings had me in a trance! The more they stretched out, the more I felt the love from them. As they got closer, the smell of sugar cookies filled the air around us. They moved and turned their heads at the same time.

My sister's guardian angel began to speak. "Hello, Keisha. How are you doing? Did you enjoy your experience with 'The Book of Life'? We are here to guide you and help you. If you have any questions, feel free to ask us."

"Can they see me?" I asked, because I couldn't see myself!

They turned in unison and said, "We can see you, Quest," ending their sentence in harmony. I noticed that as they got closer, I could hear music, so I asked, "Where is the music coming from?" They answered, "It's us Quest, that music you hear is coming from us."

What "Quest" Means

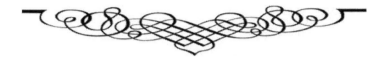

The clouds made their own music every time the wind blew. I said, "It sounds like chimes." The angels responded, "You're right, Quest." "We have questions for you." "Yes," I said. "Do you know what your name means?" I said, "Yes, the special one who was touched by heaven's light." They smiled and said, "Yes, in the physical realm, that's what Quest means. In heaven your name means 'The special one who was kissed by a rose in heaven. The special one who touched the kingdom's doors. It is you who will teach people to believe in themselves and lead them to God's glory."

"Wow! Who is going to believe me when I tell them this?" I asked. "Do you not believe what you've seen? Do you not believe what you have touched, Quest? We are angels from God's kingdom." We looked at each other eye-to-eye but no one blinked.

As my glance deepened, I said, "I believe. This is real! I'm standing here with you two angels from God's kingdom." We all held hands and I felt so loved at that moment. Everyone in heaven loves each other. I could feel love from everyone who walked past me. I felt joy and happiness all day long. If someone walked past you and said, "I love you" and hugged you, would you be offended? In heaven that's just how it is. I saw people telling others just that!

Love is exactly what the world needs, we need to love each other more. Tell someone you love them from the bottom of your heart and say it with a smile. That might change their whole day. That's what this journey was all about, that's the message I was taking back to the physical realm.

Yes! I was amazed, but more amazed because the whole time we're communicating their mouths never moved. We had been communicating through thoughts and feelings. They told me my spiritual level was brilliant for someone who hasn't passed over yet, but I knew this journey was all about my sister and I experiencing heaven together, because we used to talk about heaven when she was a child. So I was allowed to come there with Keisha to enjoy her journey.

The angels touched my little sister's wings, touching them softly and gently almost as though they meant to calm her. Now for some reason, I started noticing patterns of numbers. As a matter of fact, I realized when that began to happen that I notice patterns of numbers during very emotional experiences. The angels guided us toward a water fountain and I noticed that we all took exactly fourteen steps toward water fountain. It was so profound to me because I realized that Keisha's birthday falls on the fourteenth day of the month.

In the water fountain stood this statue and again, Keisha and I were astounded. We were grinning and laughing because the statue was of two large hands and I thought to myself in that moment, "These are God's hands!". The fountain had angels all around it pouring water on the hands of God! Just amazing! The perfect fingerprints. Touching these hands made me think about people in the world who need love need to be touched by God's glory, and how only He can care for them in a way that only He can.

I felt so at peace. It was as if God's hands moved slowly together, as if God wanted us to drink from His hands, as if to say that all of the thirsts we experience in life can only be quenched by His living water. Again, it was so peaceful to watch God's work! With all the angels around me, it seemed as though the fountain was emanating music that matched His glory. The water looked like liquid diamonds. Keisha ran her hands through the water and it was if the water flowed with life, it was a pure, untarnished moment.

There was no water on her hands at all. She did this several times as the angels looked on. They said, "Keisha, the water gives life that purifies your spirit." I asked, "Can I drink some?" They responded, "Only people who have crossed over can drink this water, Quest. It will only taste like water to you". Keisha ran her hands through the water again, and again, there was nothing on her hands! She leaned down and took a sip of the water. I could see the water going down her throat, going through her body as if it was radiant light. I asked, "What just happened? Why did the water do that to her body?" The angels said, "Her spirit is purified with heaven's water. One sip is all you need to drink, Quest." "Yeah, but the water looked clear. How did it turn blue?" I questioned.

"She's giving her spirit to God, that's why it went down blue, Quest."

I wanted experience the heavenly water, so I took a sip while the angels watched on. I just had to try it, but when I did, just like they told me, the water didn't turn blue for me. Sip after sip, nothing happened. I was so disappointed.

"We see the love you have for Keisha Quest, so, let's continue….". We looked to our right and noticed friends and family and celebrities everywhere! They started to appear from every- where, and I was so amazed. There were people everywhere, but I wasn't focused on anyone but Keisha. I noticed that she had a look of amazement on her face so I asked her what was wrong? She said, "Oh my goodness!" with a big smile on her face, "It's Marvin Gaye Big Brother! Marvin Gaye!"

"Yeah, right," I said in disbelief, I kept thinking, "My Dad's not going to believe this."

I can't believe Marvin Gaye just walked in front of me," she shouted! "Marvin! Marvin! My mom, dad, me, and my Big Brother, love you, man!"

The angels spoke, this time moving their mouths, "Keisha, you don't have to yell," acknowledging her softly. "We know you're excited, but you can just whisper. He can hear you from just a whisper."

"Hey, Marvin," she said in a whisper, "I love you!" Marvin looked at us and said, "I love you too. Welcome!" Clearly astonished, I said, "Did Marvin just speak to us and welcome us to heaven?" "Yes, Quest. He's a wonderful person," replied the angels.

Paradise Wings

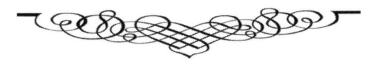

The angels turned Keisha around to adjust her wings. "Keisha, let's take your wings off and put them over here." They put them in a blue box. The box was three feet long with clouds in it as cushioning. The angels said, "If you ever want to fly around paradise, we'll give these back to you. These are the wings you use in paradise to help you do tricks in the air."

We started smelling the most pleasant smell. It was like fresh, clean laundry. We could hear wings flapping, and when we looked up, we could see the amazing butterflies.

They were larger than the butterflies in the physical realm, almost like a small bird, only more beautiful. What made this so special, is they were so brilliant, but these butterflies actually communicated with us! This is still so amazing every time I think if it!

I remember a butterfly landed on my forearm and it was just sitting there, wings still, just relaxing. It was a very special moment for me, as if we were communicating. In heaven, they fly to you, right in front our face, meeting you eye-to-eye. Their wings flap so softly, its like there's music within them. When the butterflies fly near the angels, it sounds so relaxing and loving. The music that comes from their wings makes you want to love someone. We could see ourselves in their eyes. Just mind-blowing! We stood there enjoying the music from the angels, butterflies and the clouds. The best music ever heard! It's difficult to find the right words to describe it! This brought back so many memories for us. I used to sit out front of the house and watch her admire the butterflies.

Soon the butterflies began to transform into angels and they were everywhere! "Do you see that, Keisha? Wow!" The most brilliant colors began to form in front of our eyes. We stood there taking everything in, I didn't know how I was going to remember all of this. It's like a kid remembering the best Christmas ever only a trillion times better! It's like not knowing what to expect on Christmas morning, but by the end of the day you end up getting all the gifts you ever wanted. Unreal because you just can't fathom it! But I'm here with my little sister, walking with two angels was priceless!

I'm telling you everything up there has music deep within them. I've never heard anything like it. I got so excited to touch so many angels. I can't remember how many I touched, but it felt wonderful. I put my arms out straight, took a deep breath and relaxed, letting the butterflies fly all around me. "I love this!" I said to Keisha. "I love you for bringing me here!" They all just looked at me with the same look in their eyes as if they were all happy for me to have experienced what they already knew.

It started getting foggy and all we could see were clouds. I noticed the clouds started changing colors. Then the clouds started glowing super bright and we started to see another bright light. It started looking like a tunnel and the light within it was like the sun at its hottest peak. You can't look straight at it, but in heaven, you can. It was bright, but we didn't need to blink or squint. We started walking toward the light. I started squeezing Keisha's hand tighter, as we got closer. It felt so welcoming to us. We felt love with every step we took, and it was so overwhelming that it caused us to gasp for air! The angels spoke, "You can relax. Relax! Get ready."

We didn't know what to expect next. I could feel myself starting to feel anxious like Keisha was going to leave me, so my spirit got heavy and I could feel like my eyes were starting to tear up. I thought Keisha was leaving me at that moment. She kept saying, "It's okay, Big Brother! Don't cry!" I left my little sister right there and went back to physical, where I saw myself at the table crying so hard. I was in shock as I sat at the table crying. I noticed that I'd been crying so much my shirt was drenched with my own tears.

I knew the time was getting nearer to say good-bye to my little sister. I was enjoying this journey to heaven. I didn't want to come back home to physical!

I hovered over myself at the table. As I looked up and around I saw a dazzling mist hovering over me. I could see myself shaking and crying. I wanted to cry, but you don't cry in heaven.

There's nothing but joy and happiness.

I told myself, "Quest, calm down." I said, "How can I calm down when I am losing my....?"

I felt my physical self standing up again, my shirt drenched with tears. I told myself to calm down again. I reached out to touch my own face. "Calm down. I love you." Those three words completely calmed me down. I sat back down and started taking deep breaths for myself. Again, I left my body and returned to heaven. Back in heaven, it was as though I paused a movie. We continued to walk toward the heavenly light. The angels asked me, "Are you okay, Quest?"

"Yes, why do you ask?" I inquired. "There's a tear in your eye," they responded. "Really?" and the angels reached their hands out as if they motioned for me to stop, then turned their hands around with an open palm. I saw raindrops falling into their palms, touching and disappearing. "Is it raining?" I asked. "No, these are your tears. You're fine now, Quest," they explained. Keisha said while looking at me, "They must really love you!" Turning around we could see the light directly in front of us. The female angel went through the light first, and said, "It's okay. You're here at the gates of God's kingdom." I went through the light next but noticed my clothes had changed. Keisha walked through and gasped for air. "This is how heaven looks, Big Brother!" she explained excitedly. The male angel followed, "Yes, Keisha," they said. I couldn't see anything in the beginning because my physical self had started to tear up again and it was blocking my spiritual vision. Both angels put their palms out again. As the tears began to clear up in my physical self, my vision began to improve in the spirit. White lights were everywhere. The angels instructed us to blink two times.

I blinked once, then twice. The light that was so bright and I realize that it was a reflection of the palace. We all moved toward the palace and again butterflies and doves appeared everywhere, as far as the eye could see. The sky was a special color blue. It made you feel the love that was in the atmosphere. I had never experienced anything in the physical that was this brilliant in color.

As we approached, I noticed an amazing smell of fruit and as I looked up on the glory of the entry way, I noticed beautiful swaying palm trees, butterflies flying all over the palace, and there was such a sense of magnificence. The sidewalls were so high with very large windows. There was gold trimming around the top of the palace and the walls were shimmering and sparkling with brilliance.

Roses That Love

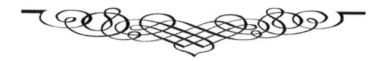

As we moved even closer toward the palace, we noticed roses in the most brilliant colors of the rainbow. These weren't just any roses. The stems were hazel and shimmered and the roses, would change colors right in front of you. I bent down to touch one of the roses and I couldn't believe how the colors seemed to dance with every touch. "Wow! Did you see that, Sis?" I asked. "Yes, I know!" she said with a laugh. "That was amazing and beautiful. The roses turned colors right in front of our faces." As I looked closer, I could feel a heartbeat from the rose. I looked at the angels and said with surprise, "Wow! Tell me that just didn't happen!?!?!" The angels explained, "Yes, Quest, it did. If your heart has love, they will feel it and that is their way of loving you!"

Wow! The most beautiful flowers just bloomed right in front of my eyes! I noticed how green the grass was and as I continued to look, I noticed stems that were dancing back and forth, just growing, then pop! The flowers just popped out and bloomed and opened up! The most brilliant, sparkling colors shot out full of beautiful glitter.

The angels told me. "Quest, that's not glitter," "It's not?" I questioned? "No, Quest! Those are love seeds. The flowers are expressing their love toward you, Quest." "What are love seeds?" I asked. "You see how the grass is that green? The flowers get happy to be in love with a new spirit. As you are the new spirit, the grass feeds off those seeds," I wanted to eat the flowers because they smelled like cotton candy. When I touched them, they turned a beautiful purple!!

"The flowers love me? How about the roses?" I asked. They told me that the roses love me too. The roses opened their petals and I could see inside them. The roses weren't just beautiful; they were actually intelligent! They bowed their heads when I walked up to them and as I leaned in to smell them, there was a rose that gently kissed my face.

That kiss felt like no other kiss I've ever received in the physical. It touched me so much that I wanted to cry just from the joy of it all. My heart was touched by a rose, literally. Whenever I would move, the rose would move with me. As I walked past the other roses, they turned the same color of the rose that kissed me. So wonderful, so heartfelt! I reached out to touch all the roses. They turned and reached out and touched me back! I could hear soft music coming from the roses. The air smelled like so many types of fruits. The palm trees were dancing, and swaying, back and forth to the music.

Amazing! My vision was normal at one moment; then I could see everything in what seemed like 3-D! The next moment I thought, should I say something or just enjoy the experience? I'm really enjoying this moment, so I'll keep it to myself.

I looked back at the roses, and they were clapping! I could see the palace starting to shimmer in color. It felt like the palace was alive and communicating with us, telling us to come closer. I was doing all of the talking and Keisha really didn't have much to say. I guess she was letting me know she'll be here forever, and because I was their guest, I got to ask the questions and observe all I could so that when I returned to the physical, I could tell the story as I saw it.

The Kingdom

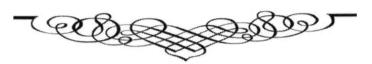

The kingdom was amazing! It didn't seem that huge coming toward it. Clouds covered half of the kingdom. That's why it didn't look so large at first. I really couldn't fathom me standing there, but here we were! As we stood outside the palace, light began to lessen, and you could see the details of the jewels in the walls of the palace. The clouds drifted away behind the palm trees. It took my breath away. From what we saw, I couldn't believe how the kingdom was built.

There aren't words to describe what I saw. The kingdom is so gorgeous! The kingdom is brilliant pure white with gold and it's so bright because the light reflects off of the jewels that the walls are made of. It seemed like the walls of God's palace were made from pure diamonds. Yes! Diamonds!

I always told Keisha how I thought the palace would look. I only went by what I read in the Bible and what pastors have told me about it. I never would have believed what I had just saw, not at all. The palace is pure white and gold all over. The roses were incredible. The front door was spectacular, it was pure gold. All the diamonds were placed in the bricks of the kingdom walls.

Yes, diamonds! All shapes and sizes. I want to say that they're made into the side of the palace, as if someone placed them one by one and side by side, like a jeweler making an expensive piece of jewelry. Every diamond known and unknown is placed on the palace walls, I touched them it was so amazing. I was just speechless at the wonder of it all.

With my spirit eyes I could see the top of the roof, all around the palace while standing in front of the palace. This surprised me because I wasn't accustomed to my eyes being able to turn around corners or see things from an aerial perspective. I never saw a door, so the question popped in my head, "How do we get in?". Next thing I remembered is that they Angels spread their wings and then I could suddenly see inside the palace. It was rather strange because I never spoke a word, I was only thinking about how to enter the palace without a door, but then the angels spoke, "We can read your thoughts, Quest." "All the time?" I wanted to know. "Yes, Quest," they said in harmony. "How about Keisha? Can she?" My little sister answered, "I can too." "Really?" I asked. "I'm pretty impressed!"

How will I remember all of this? This is too much to handle. No one's going to believe me. Tell me I'm dreaming this, so I can wake up. I can't fathom what I just saw,". "What you just saw and touched, Quest, is God's palace. We are here with you.

You will remember what you experienced when the time comes, Quest. We believe in you. The vision will be with you always. You must tell people in the physical realm what heaven really looks like and if you ever need our help, you can just call on us with your thoughts. Again, remember that we can read your mind. You can revisit heaven just by blinking, Quest. Every blink will be a glimpse of heaven at any time of the day or night, Quest," they said.

Inside The Palace

As we entered, I walked passed what looked like a library of books and it felt like just looking at a book transferred the full knowledge of the content of that book. I not only could feel the knowledge transfer into my mind, but all of the experience that went with it. It made me feel like I gained so much more knowledge than I did before just by being there. I kept thinking, wow! The longer I stay the more knowledge I gain just by being here.

As I looked around, we took ten steps into the kingdom and stopped. I don't know how I knew it was exactly 10 steps, but like I mentioned before, patterns were suddenly becoming more apparent to me now. In that moment, it felt like all the angels in the palace looked straight at us. "Are they going to greet us?" I asked. I could hear beautiful soft music playing in the background that gave of such a smooth vibration, it was like there was actual feeling in the music, unlike anything I've ever heard. Angels were everywhere and you could feel all of the love that was in the air. I felt love from every angel that I glanced at. Suddenly, they started to come toward us each with a warm smile, their smiles seemed to match Keisha's smile. I always told her that she had the warmest smile. I turned and looked at her and said, "I don't want to leave!"

Keisha replied, "I don't want to leave you, either!". "There's so much to learn up here in heaven." I said as my heart was pumping with anticipation.

I could hear the other angels talking about me. "That's Keisha's big brother, Quest. He's the special one." I heard the angels talking amongst themselves, "Who's his angel?"

I felt like royalty. I was loving it! I felt so honored. Keisha was grinning the whole time and then she said, "They really love you in heaven!".

It was mind-blowing to see all the angels at one time and then to see them in all their glory was remarkable. One moment you can see their faces and in another instance they might transform. Sometimes, Keisha and I could see our faces reflecting off of their faces and then we would see stars and then sparks that would turn into these brilliant figures of a dove or a butterfly. I was breathless because there were so many angels, so beautiful and they seemed to be waiting to be called upon.

The Love Of An Angel

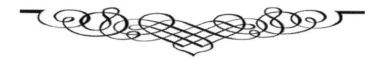

As we walked through the palace, I noticed an angel that made eye contact with me and the angel felt familiar to me. At first glance it looked like the angel was a very far distance from us, but when I took another look, within the blink of an eye, the angel was right in front of me! Stunning and Beautiful! I couldn't stop staring. I felt so much love for this angel, it was familiar like family, as if it was always with me. I didn't want the angel to leave my side.

It was like the other angels already knew this angel was there just for me. I noticed the angels that came to escort us through the heavens were assigned to my sister and I and I can remember thinking to myself, "I wonder if there are angels assigned just to me?" and it was almost as if this angel heard my thoughts and responded to my need. Once we made eye contact, I knew that angel was there for me. I looked at Keisha and she said, "How amazing is that, Big Brother?". "I'm amazed, little sis. I feel like a little kid at Christmas time! Like all of this was just for me!".

The angel approached us and then turned to me and said,

"Hello, Quest!". I asked, "How do you know my name?". As the angel answered, my little sister began laughing. "I've always been with you from time were conceived you were my assignment and I will continue to be with you always. I need you to do something for me when you get back to the physical world, I won't tell you now, but you'll know when the time is right. You will be so much happier afterwards, but for now you are good. I want you to know that I love you Quest and I always have. "That is the gift of God's love, that everyone and everything here loves naturally.

The angel looked to Keisha, and as they greeted each other, I couldn't help but hold her hand with excitement. "Hello," they said to each other. The angel could already tell what I was thinking. I was still amazed just thinking about the meaning of the angel's name.

We held hands while moving through our journey in the Kingdom. Keisha and I noticed there were no mirrors in the palace. Nowhere! I asked, "Why is that?"

The angel answered my question, "Imagine in the physical world if there were no mirrors? People wouldn't act the same way. Looks wouldn't matter. You would love a person from deep within first. It shouldn't matter how someone looks for another person to love them. It should come from your heart."

As we moved through God's mansion we came upon my sister's room. It was huge, like an apartment! Her bed and pillows were made of clouds, her sheets and pillowcases were silky. Our family pictures were there sitting on her dresser. There were photos of her kids and of a child she lost years ago, and I was in awe because I had never seen the child before because Keisha lost her in the first trimester. Now that I'm thinking back, the baby angel that flew past us when we were standing at the front door was the same baby in the photo. I noticed that a high school picture of little sis was there, too, sitting posted by her bed. Her room was a soft pink with windows that overlooked the dancing palm trees. Wow! "Keisha, how wonderful is this?" I heard the chimes, and clapping, harps, horns blowing,

"If I hear chimes, does that mean someone passed over?" I asked. "Yes," she answered. "They have passed over and their spirit has traveled, and they have finally made it here to heaven." My hands were just kissed by my angel as if to be happy for me to come into this knowledge of something so sacred.

I knew my time in heaven was coming to an end because I felt emotion rising inside which was a trigger for me to see myself in the physical. So once again, I turned my focus to almost look for myself in the physical world, and again I could see myself back in the physical world and it made my eyes start to tear up. I remembered what the angels taught me about how to refocus myself so I could stay in the spiritual realm, just like it happened in the beginning of our journey and I was able to snap myself back into the moment. My instincts were so sharp and I became more aware of the training the angels gave me and I began to understand that they were preparing me for battle. I realized that I had been given power! Spiritual power! I felt invincible like there was nothing anyone could do to me in the physical world that would not make me love them. I felt unconditional love! My spirit had changed. I've always been a loving person, but now, I really feel a genuine desire to just love everyone. I had been personally trained by angels from God's glory how to do battle in the spirit and I now saw heaven as being my home in the spirit.

I've always felt like I could read people's thoughts as a kid. I felt that by looking into their eyes, I could find their spirit and feel some of their emotions and even some of their needs.

I can remember sometimes that I could see a mist of smoke hovering over people, but now, I understand that it wasn't just a mist of smoke, but an angel hovering over them who just wanted to help that person. I could feel people's energy and sadness. I could not explain why I felt this way. At times throughout my life, I could see spirits and talk with them, its different than when you walk and talk with people in the physical realm, but when it happens, it feels just as familiar. I could see a glowing realm around someone sometimes and I just somehow knew that it meant they were about to cross over to the spirit realm. I now know what to look for and I can tell when I need to help people. I don't go around looking for people to help, I just know when I'm supposed. God places them in front of me and I get a familiar feeling from them, and it's up to me to tell that person what I've seen or what's God wants me to tell them at that time.

If you summon an angel, they will come, but it is you who must believe spiritually. They are here to help us, to enlighten us, communicate with us through our five senses: sight, sound, smell, taste, touch and of course through our thoughts as well, Take all the negative thoughts and turn them into positive ideas.

I do like seeing angels now, but before I didn't! I was in

denial. I can tell you whether you have an angel around you or not. I meet people and I just want to show them love. It's like I can feel if they have pain that needs to be healed in their souls and its intuitive to want to heal the pain with love so that all you see is the beauty in them. If I could, I would touch everyone in the world with love, joy and happiness in their hearts, I would do it right now. I feel that because my hands have touched God's holy water, the diamonds on the walls of the palace, my hands having been kissed by an angel, and having touched the hands of God has left an anointing on me. God told me that we should believe that it is possible for each of us to make a change in the world, one person at a time if we just take the time to look in the mirror and love ourselves first.

My instincts were tingling and as the angels escorted us I could hear a very frightening roar. I stood in front of Keisha to protect her. This roar sent deep chills through my body. Keisha wasn't even afraid! All her fears were gone so seeing her calm, I began to feel calmer as well. I kept repeating to myself, "No fear! Just believe, no fear!" That's all I kept thinking.

The roar became intense. I was looking straight ahead to see where the roar was coming from. Again, I stood in front of my little sister with caution because I didn't know where the roaring was coming from. "I'm okay, Big Brother. Thanks!" she said.

A white tiger appeared. He didn't look that happy. "Why is he roaring so loud?" I asked.

The angels responded, "He's not loud Quest, you're hearing him with your physical senses. If you calm yourself, the tiger will calm itself." As I calmed myself, the tiger was calming down. The angel motioned for the tiger to come towards it. The tiger and I connected eye-to-eye. The tiger started running toward us, roaring. The tiger was about a hundred feet from us. He was HUGE! Then he jumped in the air toward us!

I wondered why he jumped from so far away, a hundred foot leap! At that moment my vision was the same way as if I were back at my house, looking at that bird. I could zoom in and out, top and bottom, at the same time. The tiger and I glanced eye-to-eye, as he began to approach. Because my senses were so high, I could see straight through the tiger. I saw all the pretty stripes. His coat was beautiful. He jumped in the air again toward us and I slowed his motion, stopping him in midair, and walking under him! I could touch his teeth, hair, nose, ears, tail, paws, claws, and his chest.

As he continued in slow motion, I stood by my little sister along with Keisha's angels beside us. The tiger landed and walked toward us. His head was very HUGE. His body was ten feet long! I stepped forward, but he didn't want me to come near him. But I felt a connection with this tiger. He bypassed me and walked right up to Keisha. She bent down toward the tiger's face. I was thinking how he could have bitten her whole face off, but he wasn't just any tiger. My little sister whispered to her angels, "I've seen those eyes before."

"Yes, Keisha, you have. You've seen those eyes your whole life," the angels responded.

"I don't understand," she said, looking so confused. I noticed the tiger had a mole on his cheek bone, under his right eye. "How pretty is that?" I asked.

She said, "I get to look at you every day." "Me?" I asked my little sister's angels, but before I couldn't finish getting my sentence out, they answered me!

"Yes, you, Quest." I looked at Keisha because I was really confused then. At that time, I heard rumbling in the air. As we looked up, there were clouds in the palace. Breath taking, purple clouds that sparkled. Keisha said, "Oooooh! Now I know where I saw this tiger before your house, Big Brother! On your wall!" "Oh, that's right, Keisha! Girl, now you're thinking!" I said.

"Not only the picture on the wall, but if you look really close at the tiger, his face looks like your brother's, face. If your brother were an animal, he would be a tiger. That's why the tiger bypassed him earlier, it was as if he were looking at himself." explained Keisha's angels.

"Hello, my son!" I heard this very deep voice greeting me. "Is that the clouds?"

"Yes, Quest, it's God." My mind went blank! I looked at my sister and God spoke again,

"Hello my child. Welcome home." I stood there shaking my head back and forth. "Wow! Wow!"

God spoke to me, "My son, Keisha brought you to the kingdom so that you could experience it and see that it was real. It is I who am giving you the gift and ability for you to tell others what you've experienced here in heaven. What I have shown you, others will be envious and jealous of, my son. So keep your faith! Believe in yourself, always. I've shown you my kingdom and want you to tell people whom I bring into your life that heaven is real. Share the glory of the experience with others who will be blessed by knowing it because it will bring them hope, joy, happiness, and love." "I will, God. I will help people you bring into my life."

Devine Guidance

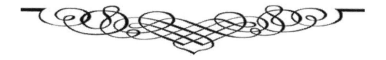

God then turned his focus toward Keisha. "Keisha, my child, I love you and I am giving you this tiger. It is now your animal and you must care for it."

Keisha and I looked at each other in amazement! I could feel my vision getting blurry again as I started feeling anxiety that this whole experience was about to be over. I started to feel sad in my body and I felt the emotion welling up inside as the thought of all of this being over began to creep into my spirit. It was just like the other times, it started blocking my spiritual connection.

At that time, I kissed her on the cheek and said, "Thank you so much for bringing me with you. I don't really want to go back. I'm going to miss you so much! How long have we been up here in heaven?"

All the angels turned their heads toward us and said in harmony, "There is no time in heaven Quest." I could see the clock in my house from heaven. The time was 8:21. That's one hour in the physical, but it didn't seem like it. They said, "You are a quick learner. There will be more to learn in the physical, Quest. Keisha can show you and teach you other things, you will need to know, and if she doesn't know, you can always ask your angel."

At that moment I felt like crying in heaven. No one cries in heaven because there's nothing but joy. My eyes started blinking and started tearing up because I started to feel like I our time together was coming to an end, then I felt myself drifting away. Keisha consoled me, "It's okay, Big Brother. I'm okay now. God is with me and I am home."

I could feel my spirit slowly coming back to the physical realm. I hugged my little sister and her angels and kissed all of their cheeks. I could feel their love and I could tell they did not want me to leave.

As I backed away from them, then the palace, back through the garden, I saw my beautiful rose on the way back and she reached out to me with her petal to give me a kiss on my cheek. I could feel her love and longing for me to stay as well.

My little sister and her angels stood back while I moved toward some brilliant orange clouds. A rainbow drifted over the palace, as if the palace was saying good-bye to me. My little sister said, looking over her shoulder with a single tear in her eye, "Big Brother, I love you so much. I will always have you by my side in the spirit. I don't want to say good-bye, but I'm not there in the physical realm anymore and as much as this pains me to say, you must say good-bye to me for now. I am at peace and there's no more pain. You must understand and love me in the spirit. Tell Mom and Dad that I love them with all my heart. I gained great strength from mom and the artistic senses from dad! What a wonderful combination! Without you all, I wouldn't have been me! May your lives continue to be filled with blessings, I love you." My mind went blank. I could feel my heart slow down and feel the decent of returning to the physical realm. Losing a loved one or someone dear to you really makes you think about life, the good memories, and laughter. Just standing there in heaven with my little sister was a blessing from God. I didn't want to leave her. "Wait! Please teach me more. Can I stay just a couple of minutes more? Please, Keisha, don't go! I love you so much! Wait! Please God! Please tell me it's not over!"

I could feel myself backing out of the spiritual realm and as I drifted, I could see Keisha was moving toward the front doors, walking with the tiger, rubbing his head, and both angels were trailing behind her.

"Wait, don't go!" I begged. My little sister, looked back over her shoulder, calling to me,

"Big Brother, I'm gonna be up here for a while. Tell everyone I love them!

"Don't Go, Keisha! I love you so much. What am I supposed to do without you? Please God!". I was overwhelmed with emotions as I drifted back to physical realm, falling back through the clouds.

I looked back and saw Keshia waving and saying, "Big Brother! I love you too! I'll see you in heaven!"

"Keisha! Don't do this to me," I could feel my spirit crying out. It felt as if I was falling out of the sky, like my arms were limp, and I could feel the air on my back. My head and my body were motionless. I had my eyes closed because I just didn't care to think about the experience coming to an end at that moment. Everything I've learned in heaven was racing through my mind so fast. The thought of the time I spent with my little sister made my heart even sadder because I know it will be a while before I get to see her again. I could feel my physical body full of emotion and crying so loud. Even though no one could hear me, all I could think about was begging God," Please let me bring my sister back with me. Please don't do this to me. I love her so much," I prayed. My last thought was my little sister running toward me with her arms outstretched with this big smile on her face, so happy to see me!

I could see my house as I drifted back, but I didn't want to come back. As I was falling, my spiritual instincts kicked in and I could feel myself returning to the physical realm. It's overwhelming for me now just to remember leaving her again. It takes my breath away and makes me pause to let the emotion pass through me.

As I continued to fall, I closed my eyes. Then, out of nowhere I heard, "Big Brother, open your eyes." Then I heard it again "Quest, open your eyes." As my eyes slowly opened, Keisha and my angel were together calling my name, "Quest!" They appeared with a mist of sparkling colors. Then I saw a burst of beautiful stars. Keisha appeared to have larger wings. She wasn't wearing this in heaven. I remember her wings being spread out and they were silver in color. It was as if they appeared out of the clouds to rescue me as I was falling. I closed my eyes with my arms and body going limp. I passed out for a second. I could hear their voices calling my name over and over, "Quest, wake up! Quest wake up! Believe, Quest! We are here to rescue you!" I woke up and could see them coming faster and faster. "We got you, Quest! We won't let you fall, but you are going back to the physical realm Quest."

"I love you so much Keisha, why would I want to return home? Why?" I asked. Keisha responded, "We will always be here for you, Quest."

I didn't realize that I was already home, standing in my living room. They could see the physical body sitting at the table crying. My angel placed her hand on my shoulders, leaned down and said, "Quest, you will be okay. I love you. Keisha loves you so relax and breathe. We love you."

I Believe

Remember everything I have shown you. Only certain parts of this experience will remain fresh in your mind. When you start to write this experience, to share this with the world, it is only then you will remember everything I have shown you. With every blink you will see heaven like you've seen it before, only more intensely. Your handwriting will change, for it is not only you that is writing this experience; you're writing this experience with your angel with the help of the Holy Spirit. Do not question yourself. Write it as you see it. It will come to you. Take care, my son". I responded, "God, I do believe,"

    I held my head down at the table. When I looked up, my spirit walked toward me, then stepped into my body. I felt very happy and full of love. I stopped crying, now because all I could feel at this point was full of love.

    When I returned to my body, I knew I felt different, but at first, I thought that maybe I had fallen asleep and dreamed all of this.

    Then God spoke, "My son, don't worry what people

think of you. So many people, family and friends, are going to envy you, for what I have shown you. They will believe you. I will place people in your life for you to share this heavenly experience with. If they don't believe you, they will come back to you one day when I bring it back to their remembrance. Be ready, my son. Look them in their eyes and connect with their spirit. It is you whom I have chosen to share with people about my glory. It is you my son, that believes and has faith. You will not remember everything I have shown you. Only certain parts of this experience will remain fresh in your mind. When you start to write this experience, to share this with the world, it is only then you will remember everything I have shown you. With every blink you will see heaven like you've seen it before, only more intensely. Your handwriting will change, for it is not only you that is writing this experience; you're writing this experience with your angel with the help of the Holy Spirit. Do not question yourself. Write it as you see it. It will come to you. Take care, my son". I responded, "God, I do believe."

At The Table

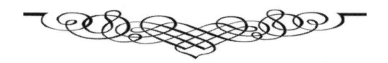

When I became conscious again, I was aware that I was now back in my body and it felt like my senses were heightened and I started immediately noticing things, like why is my shirt so wet? Why was I warm and sweating? I realized that my physical body was crying so much while I was out of my body that I wasn't sweating, it was all tears. I was overwhelmed as I sat at the table trying to accept that I just had that experience! My mind was so far gone as I relived everything, I thought, I must be hallucinating! I looked at the time, I even checked the date. I didn't know what to do. So I got up and I took a shower and got dressed. Then, I woke my son and nephew up. I couldn't believe they were asleep this whole time!

I could hear my little sister's voice, so faintly, "I told you I had that under control!"

"So, I wasn't hallucinating," I said to her. "No," she said.

"So, why can I still hear you?" "Because I'm here with you," Keisha answered. "I've come back to train you. "Train me? On what? I thought I was finished?" "No, Big Brother, I have to teach you about numbers and what they mean. Also, about clouds and stars." "Really? How long is that going to take," I wanted to know.

"Seven days," she responded. "Why seven days? I'm still kind of lost about the whole heaven experience. Why do I feel like I know so much, but I can't explain it?". "It'll all come back to you when you start writing the book." "What book?" I asked a little bewildered. "The book! Your day in heaven," she replied. "I'm going to write a book?" I questioned. "Yeah, right! People are going to think I'm crazy or I'm hallucinating the whole story?"

"Story? This is real, Big Brother. Who do you think you're talking to?" Keisha asked. A part of me didn't want to believe that this experience was real. As I stood in my hallway, I could hear my little sister's voice behind me saying, "If you're listening to me, then you believe that you're talking to me. Why not believe that I'm behind you?" she said even before I could turn around. As I turned around, the hallway had so many little stars, like white Christmas lights on a tree. Her body was glowing. I could see her face. I realize now, in hindsight, that it was the Holy Spirit showing itself to me in a form that I wouldn't be scared of so that I could receive my assignment and continue trusting the guidance that I was receiving.

The Teaching Begins

I walked back in my room startled that I could still hear Keisha speaking to me. Keisha went on to tell me that over the next seven days she would teach me about clouds, numbers, and stars and about how I could communicate with the angels. She went on to tell me that my angel would teach me how to hear music in the air and to use my spiritual connection at a higher level.

I walked out from my room thinking my son and nephew probably heard everything Keisha was telling me, but they didn't. I really wish they could have experienced what I went through. This heaven experience would be much easier to explain to them if they had, but they didn't. The fact that I didn't say anything to them, and I kept it to myself didn't make it any easier to be able to explain to anyone about that experience.

Keisha left my presence just as quickly as she came. She was gone now. I was still in disbelief. My thoughts were: seven days of training; the angel experience; God; the palace; flying through clouds, the ocean water; the dolphins. As I sat there, I couldn't remember much more than that. I was very happy to have experienced heaven, but now what? I had to tell my family now, but how? I was concerned and said so out loud as if Keisha was still in my presence, and when I did so, I heard Keisha's voice respond, "I'll be with you, Big Brother, when you tell them, okay?". "Why do you think Ma and Dad are going to believe me, Keisha?" I asked.

"Trust me, they will!" she answered.

Keisha came to me and began to teach me all about clouds and what relevance to us is. All I ever knew about clouds is what I'd learned in school. She began to teach me that angels sometimes use clouds to show us things. We just don't pay them any attention. She explained, "When your spirit is in alignment with God, you can hear music when you look to the clouds. Some- times, you can see the faces of your loved ones. I've even seen a "rainbow cloud". They're beautiful! Thanks to my little sister, I see them all the time. So now I know when I hear music in the air, I know there are angels close to the clouds in the sky. Before Keisha died, I could hear music in the air. I just couldn't explain it. I heard chimes and horns the most. Everything else I heard, I can't explain the type of instruments that the sounds may have come from. Every time I hear chimes, I think about her. Sometimes I wake up to chimes playing in the air. It's so relaxing and beautiful to hear. Now that my spirit is clear I hear the music in the air and it is so clear.

Keisha also began to teach me about how angels communicate with you through numbers. It was really profound to me that when my little sister passed away, I kept seeing the numbers 7*2*3* and 2*1*8. These numbers we burned into my mind to the point where I noticed one day that the watch

I was wearing during the out of body experience stopped at 7:23! Another example, I remember going to the store to buy a newspaper and some gum, and it was ironic that the total purchase with taxes was $2.18 (2*1*8). I still didn't understand why I kept running into these numbers or what they meant but I was noticing this same pattern coming up in everything. Another example is when I realized that my little sister's apartment door was the seventh door on her floor and that there were exactly twenty- three steps (7*2*3) from the front door of the building to her apartment. Now at the time, I didn't even know why these numbers were relevant but Keisha said she would explain it all to me another time. Keisha would also show me how the stars were relevant at a later time as well.

Mom, I Have Something To Tell You......

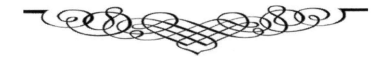

The day had come for me to tell my family what I had experienced. I remember it was February 21, 2009. God told me to do so, so I knew I had to be obedient. I was talking to God on the ride over to my parents house asking Him how I should go about doing this because I had no clue how I was even going to start the conversation. I heard God say, "Quest, my son, have your mother sit down and take a deep breath. Tell her ,"..it's because what I'm about to tell you is a little unbelievable". God said, "Your heaven experience will touch her heart and others. This will be relief to your mother's grief and will make her soul and heart feel so beautiful. Look your mother directly in her eyes when you tell her about this event."

I was so excited as I pulled up. I went up to the house, and all my brothers and sisters were there. My dad came in the house just as I had entered.

After I explained my experience to the family, my mother

looked at me and said, "I knew you were special, like some kind of medium. That explains to me all those other times too, that you had angels with you all those years ago. I knew it! Now this all makes sense to me. You and Keisha were special, like mediums or angels. Keisha could foresee what was going to happen to people." I said, "Ma, I've been in denial for years about my gift. I thought I was crazy as a kid. I could feel people around me, sometimes seeing them in my dreams, but they weren't dreams. I know that now." I hugged my mother and said, "I love you, Ma! I know that Keisha is okay now." As I shared my heavenly experience with my family, they all had the same look on their faces – eyes wide opened and mouth slightly opened like they were saying, "Aaaaah!". It was like this was my "coming out about my spiritual experience" to my whole family. My parents had known I was different as a child. I knew I was, too. I was just in denial for years. As I shared my experience, Keisha was there in the house looking right at me. She was standing by my mother first, then my dad. I stopped talking because I thought they could see her. My event was short from what I could remember. Granted the family was amazed, they asked a whole lot of questions. Lord, they had so many questions to ask me! I really felt this experience brought each of us closer as a family. Our love was now stronger than ever.

    I felt that my "Seven Days" of learning had now begun. As I drove over to my parents' house, I noticed the same cloud had followed me. I kept seeing the same numbers pass by me, 7/23/218. When I went to the store on my way there, the total of my purchases was $2.18. I put gas in my truck at Pump #7.

When I parked my truck in front of my parent's house, I took twenty-three steps from my truck to the front door.

I felt amazing after telling the whole family what Keisha asked me to tell them. It was like I was being obedient to the Holy Spirit. It just felt right. Even though this huge burden was lifted though, I was still battling the anxiety of having to go the church, view her body in the coffin, and ultimately watch her body be returned to the earth. This caused me a lot of anxiety, but at some point, I just took a deep breath and it was almost like I breathed in the Holy Spirit and suddenly, I had a calmness and a peace that surpassed ALL of my understanding.

In the days that followed, all of the plans were finalized and we knew what day we were going to funeralize her. We decided that we would all wear purple, so I picked out what I was going to wear that day. I didn't know what to expect, but I started to feel some anxiety again and every time I felt it, I could hear Keisha saying, "It's ok Big Brother, it's ok". The night before her services, I couldn't really sleep because I just didn't know how things were going to go.

The morning of, we were all in route and I remember the song "Halo" by Beyonce came on and I started to cry, but when I looked in the mirror to wipe my tears, but it was as if I felt Keisha was there wiping them away and saying to me that I needed to be strong for her son and mine.

Arriving at the church, we got out of the car and started walking toward the door. We walked in and greeted family members, and we were greeted by one of the assistants about moving in to view the body and as we moved toward that room, my feet just froze at the entryway. It literally felt like I had on cement shoes, like I just couldn't walk forward! My son Devin asked me if I was ok? I replied, "Yeah, I'm good…….I just feel like I can't move!". As my feet started to move, it felt like I was dragging bricks on my feet walking up to the casket. I literally started to feel exhausted. I made it to the front of the pews, but it wasn't where I wanted to sit, because it felt like I had just run a race with my feet dragging, so I sat down at the first place we came to in the front pew.

Lost Without My Sister......

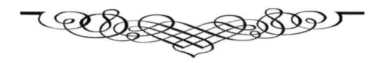

Sitting there in the pew with my other family members, I remember zoning out when people started walking passed me to view the body asking if I was okay. All I heard was "Yeah, we're here if you need us, okay?" But, when my mother, father, or Ty came near, I lost it! I started crying uncontrollably. I knew our family wouldn't be the same after this day. I felt like my heart taken from me and I couldn't find it. No one could ever find my heart again, no one! Lost! I Lost my Heart!

When you love someone with your heart, it's a pure love. I loved what Keisha and I shared. It was special. A little sister is a good friend for life and I just lost a good friend for life! Lost!

I would let her win when we would race, just so I could hear her laugh! I remember bringing her a lollipop because she was putting her makeup on for the first time, looking like a clown, but she didn't know that. She just trusted me. When I used to go pick her up from daycare, she would come running out of the school, arms outstretched smiling from ear to ear. "Big Brother," she would call, "Big Brother!" Just like she hadn't seen me all year. "I have so much to show you, look what I made for you today!"

As I prepared myself to view my little sister's body, I could hear her quietly talking to me. My spirit and I was feeling sadder then and I started to cry. My uncle Jake was my escort. He understood my grief because he had lost his son, Spike, ten years ago to gun violence. I love him for being there with me. I'm not a small person and my uncle is much shorter and smaller than I am, but he was solid as a rock to me in that moment as he held me up and consoled me. As I approached her casket, my crying intensified, my body became numb, and my legs turned into rubber. My head bent backwards like I was going to faint. My little sister's voice said, "Oh, no you're not, Big Brother! I need you to be strong so others can draw their strength from you."

I approached the casket. My uncle Jake encouraged me, "Come on, man, be strong!"

I cried, "I can't bear to see her like this." My little sister asked, "No, you have to see me Big

Brother! I'm your sister." I could feel my heartbeat slowing down. I knew I wasn't going to make it.

"I'm not going to make it. I'm so sorry, Keisha. I'm not going to make it. My heart is in too much pain," I lamented. I really began to feel my heartbeat and I could see Uncle Jake's son, Spike, helping him hold me up. I knew that I wasn't going to make it. I was dying right in front of my little sister. My vision became hazy. All I saw was white.

I could hear my heart slowing down. Bump, bump, bump. My uncle Jake said, "Hey man! Have a seat." I heard my heartbeat. It wasn't normal and I needed help. My uncle didn't know that, but I knew. My vision became blurrier, but I could still hear. My uncle Jake didn't know what state I was in. My eyes were slightly closed, I was looking at the slide show of my sister. As I sat there in shock, Keisha said, "Hey, Big Brother! Remember these pictures? Just like in heaven."

"It's too much to handle, Keisha I'm sorry. I'm sorry. I love you, Mom, Dad, and Ty, I'm sorry," is all I could say. As I sat there motionless, no one knew anything. I heard my uncle's voice say, "Take a rest, son." My sister started shouting, "Please! Someone help my brother! Not my brother! Not today!"

Angels stood by her casket, some were big and some were small. "Please help my big brother!" Ty pleaded. One angel answered, "He'll be saved today. He will."

Ask For An Angel

I can hear you, Keisha! I need an angel to come help me!" I screamed! I could smell the angel approaching. I heard him with a strong voice, "SIT UP, Quest! Take a deep breath. God has sent me to help you." I stood up, crying. Whoosh! This angel came down in front of me. He stood right there in front of me, moving toward me. "I'm here for you, Quest. Take a deep breath. Your heart is not well. There's only one thing I can do." "What's that," I asked. He turned around and I began to smell sugar cookies in the air. I asked him, "What's next?" He took a step backwards, his hair touching my nose, then walked through me. He put his wings straight out. I felt energized to the max, like being shocked, but this was all love. "Take a deep breath, Quest." My breathing became more normal, and my heartbeat was normal. As I walked toward my sister's casket, I kept touching my face, left side, then the right side. His feathers were touching my face. He put his wings straight out, all sixteen feet, straight out. No one walked past me. I still couldn't look at my little sister in that lovely casket that she was laying in. I walked past it, taking the first chair I saw, my uncle by my side. An angel spoke to me, "Quest, take deep breaths for me.

With every breath, you will have a good memory of your sister. I complied and began to feel stronger with every breath I took. My vision was intact. I could see clearly again. "Stand up by yourself, Quest."

My uncle looked and spoke, "You sure you can handle this by yourself, son?"

"Yes, I feel good," I said with a smile. I got up and could feel everyone looking at me. I could hear their thoughts. I knew that I was okay, walking to the open casket, smiling as I went along. I could feel my little sister giving me hugs and kisses just like when she was five years old again. I started laughing and smiling, holding her hand. An angel stood in back of me, with his wings spread apart. No one walked up at all. This was my healing time. I said, "Thank you, Keisha, for what you've done for me. I've lost you in the physical, but I can be with you every day in the spiritual world."

Keisha was still hugging me, and not wanting to let me go.

Keisha said, "I know Big Brother.

I had to come back and get you so you could experience heaven with me."

As I left her casket, I turned to my mother, and gave her a hug for Keisha and myself.

"I'm okay, Ma! And so is she! I love you, Ma!". I sat in my chair and heard all this cheering, music and clapping. I knew that my job here was done. I became joyful and super calm. As I looked over at Keisha's casket, I saw two angels and the said "We're so happy and joyful for you, Quest. Keisha is very happy for you too! "You're welcome, Quest." Then they all flew away. I heard a soft voice with beautiful celestial music playing, "Hello, Quest.", "Don't be afraid, I'm here to help. This is one of the things I was talking about you doing once you get back to the physical realm" the angel said to me.

One Last Tear

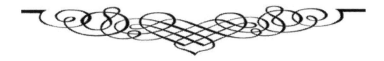

In her right hand, she placed it over my heart. Her left hand softly wiped my tears away. She said, "I'm okay now, Big Brother. You don't have to cry for me anymore. Hey, we went to heaven together, just like we said we were going to do. Remember?" With tears streaming down my face, hiding behind my sunglasses, I got up one last time before the casket closed. I leaned down with tears and kissed Keisha on her cheek. I noticed my tears touched her face. As they rolled down her face, it looked like her last tear. As I returned to my seat, I felt a peace that surpassed my understanding, but I was calm, really calm after that. As the casket was closed the Minister began to read Keisha's eulogy.

I walked back over to view the casket a couple more times. I couldn't bear to even look at her. I remembered my legs feeling like rubber. I heard later that an angel was helping me by carrying me to and from the casket. All I kept doing was wiping my face, left and right in his feathers. He had one wing spread straight out and the other around me, like he was giving me time to heal. When I started to calm down and relax, the angel left my side.

He looked over his shoulder and said, "You're okay now, Quest. If you need me, call me. We're always here to help you, Quest."

As my little sister lay there in this beautiful white and gold casket, I knew my time was limited from seeing her once more. I could hear the soft music in the background getting louder. It was time to close the casket. To see my beautiful sister lying there dead and motionless, and knowing this is it, this would be the last time I could ever see my sister and feel my sister. When Minister Stanton asked if anyone wanted to be saved and have Jesus come into their hearts and forgive them of all their sins. I sat waiting. I told myself I was already saved. But I wasn't. That's when I saw a small angel with wings, flying and hovering over my brother and I. I saw my brother jump as if someone tried to pick him up. I could feel my suit jacket lift up as if the Holy Spirit was encouraging me to get up. So I got up and walked over to Minister Stanton, looking him in his eyes, I could feel his spirit. "Good," he said. Here came my brother. My son, my sister's kids, my cousin (that I haven't seen in twenty years), and Keisha's daughter's father. We all stood holding hands, embracing one another. We asked for forgiveness, prayed, and it felt amazing and each of us knew that our names were now in God's Book of Life. I stood there and

I could feel his genuinity and love. Thank you so much, I love you for guiding me, and helping me to start a new life, Minister Stanton.

Leaving the church, my mind was thinking about "723." I don't know why I was thinking of those numbers. As we entered the cemetery, I felt my attention turning toward a life size statue of Jesus and I really felt drawn to it, but we were headed to my sister's gravesite and as it turns out, my sister's gravesite was actually in the direction of the statue.

When we arrived at the gravesite, I stood there and started crying uncontrollably until it felt like I cried out all of the tears I had. I took a flower off her casket, and just held it as if she had given it to me. I felt a wind blow and it was as if my spirit was at peace again.

"723" stuck in my head. "I need help with this one, Keisha, I'm stuck," I said. Keisha said,

"I can't think about numbers now, but I'll tell you later."

Prayer ended and we all went back to the church for the repass. I sat by my mother at the table, feeling really happy and joyful. I wanted to thank everyone for coming to show my little sister some love. So as I passed everyone, I said, "I love you all. Thank you so much for coming."

As we left the church and went back to my parents' house, I wanted to tell everyone about my experience in heaven, but I didn't. I stayed to myself and sat by my mother all evening. My little sister was there standing beside my mother the whole time. I noticed a haziness around my Mother, but I wondered why no one could see this hazy mist behind her. So, I took a picture of my mother sitting there. The sunlight beamed through the curtains making my mother's shadow appear, but at the instance that I took the picture, because my little sister was standing behind her, there was no shadow appearing at that moment. As the day was coming to an end, I knew I should share this event with others, but something in my spirit told me not to do it then.

The numbers "723" still kept coming up. By this time, I had told my family that this number was stuck in my head since the funeral and it had the whole family wondering, "What was the meaning of 723?". It stayed on everyone's mind every day and every night!

One day following the burial, I felt the Holy Spirit calling me to go back to visit the gravesite, so I complied and went to visit. That's when I felt the instruction to walk toward a cross that was sitting close to Keisha's gravestone. In doing so, I literally counted exactly twenty-three steps away! So, be encouraged to pay attention to simple details when your loved one passes away. Notice the time; their house address; license plate number; their age; when you go to the store, the total of your purchase, and the change from the purchase. You might be surprised that you may start noticing a pattern of numbers constantly standing out to you.

On my sister's birthday, I went with my Mom & Dad to visit Keisha's gravesite and they were concerned because it snowed. They didn't know how they were going to find the gravesite, but I remembered my little sister's resting place is exactly 23 steps from the side of the cross located in the graveyard. It really made me smile, of course they were wondering why I was smiling so hard, but I knew exactly where it was because of the numbers 7*2*3 and what it meant, and it was 2:18 p.m. when we were standing next to her gravesite. What a wonderful way to celebrate her birthday and know that her spirit was with us.

Surprise Me

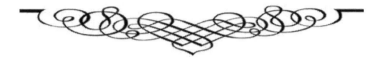

My parents decided to leave and I stayed behind to just spend a little more time thinking about my little sister. As I stood there meditating on the many memories we shared together, she appeared and asked me, "You want to see something that will blow your mind, Big Brother?". I thought what could possibly blow my mind at a cemetery? But I indulged her and said, "Yeah, show me!" I heard a scream that sounded like a woman. Then the scream got louder! As I walked toward where I thought I heard the scream I walked away from the gravesite and started moving through some bushes on the edge of the cemetery property. Then Keisha appeared again and asked, "You see that?" "Yes! A peacock!" I said. I had never seen a peacock in person before, so it really surprised me, but there it was, right here in right in front of us. As I opened my palm, it came right to me. At every step it took toward me, I became calmer. It was like he was communicating with me.

My little sister asked me, "Close your hand." As I did, it stopped. "Watch this," she said.

WHOOSH! The peacock's feathers opened up in front of my eyes. I touched them softly. This made me remember when I went to heaven I saw all those angels and I was in awe when I saw them open their wings. It was pretty amazing to watch.

As I drove home, I was thinking about how I didn't believe in angels at first, and I remembered how some months before my sister's death, I fell asleep with the TV on and I heard an infomercial come on and I could hear people talking about angels. Then the TV's sleep timer shut it down. Suddenly, the TV turned back on all by itself and I remember thinking about how weird that was and then whoever was speaking at the time asked the question, "Do you believe in angels?". It was really ironic, but I couldn't explain how that happened, so I was just in awe again! This show was on for thirty minutes. While I slept, I envisioned everything they were talking about. This time I got up to look at it. How? Who turned my TV on? I was convinced that an angel did because just like in my visit to heaven, whenever angels are around the smell like sugar cookies and smoke always seems to be present and I could smell that in the air so I knew there had to be an angel in my presence. I watched the show and was amazed because it taught me a lot about what to notice if I sensed an angel's presence that most people would overlook.

I am a pretty upbeat person, but whenever I would feel a little down, I would call to speak with my little sister about my feelings. Often times, I would come to find out, she was going through the same thing. We would start laughing. I'd crack a joke just to hear her laugh and that would make me feel so much better, comforted, and loved. From that, I learned that we should always call someone you love when you're feeling down and depressed. Love makes the heart smile.

When my sister passed away, she would communicate with me more in the daytime, but I couldn't feel her presence the same way at night. Sometimes I could see her face in the clouds during the day but, I would feel so low when it started to get dark knowing that I had to wait until the sun came up again the next morning in order to feel close to her again. It's funny because one day I heard my little sisters' voice saying, "Nope! I'm with you all the time, it's just that you can't see me in the stars at night. I'm going to show you how to connect with me at night though. Remember when I told you that I would teach you about the clouds, the numbers, and the stars? Well here's your lesson about the stars" Keisha told me that I should pick a clear night when the stars were shining brightly. Then she said to clear my mind, take deep breaths, and I focused on only happy thoughts. I didn't know what affect the experience was going to have on me, but I was anxious to see how I would feel. So the first time I tried the "Face in the Stars" experience, I did exactly as she instructed. I picked a clear night when the stars were shining brightly, I made sure that I had a good camera to capture the whole thing, then I then cleared my mind, took some deep breaths, and I focused on only happy thoughts of my little sister. Then, I pointed the camera toward the stars, I put my finger on the button, and when I opened my eyes, I clicked the flash button. It was then that I saw her face in the stars! I was completely astounded. I did it over and over again. Then I showed it to my mother, brothers, and sisters and they were amazed too. It was another experience that we shared together to feel close to her and that we could each use whenever we wanted to feel close to her. It really made my mother feel relieved that she could still feel her baby's presence whenever she wanted on any given clear night.

Three Crosses

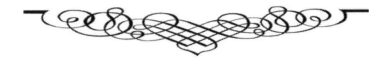

I remember another time when I was out with my family and we were headed out to go grab something to eat not far from my Mother's house. When we got inside of the restaurant, we ordered, and I suddenly felt Keisha's presence. I felt very uncomfortable because I didn't want to make a spectacle of myself, but then I heard Keisha's voice! I heard my little sister's voice telling me to video tape the sunset". Keisha said, "Watch how the video turns out. It's going to amaze you." I was trying figure out if any of them could hear her as well, but no one seemed to indicate that they could so I was hesitant to respond to her. So I ignored her. I heard her giggle, and then she said, "Are you avoiding me?", then she giggled again and I didn't reply, I just acted as if nothing was happening. I thought I saw my son looking at me like he could see or hear her also, but I didn't want to look at him because then I'd have to explain it and I just wasn't comfortable doing that in that moment. So in my spirit I responded like, "Not now, please, not right now!". I could hear her say, "Oh, ok, I'll get your attention!". I was sitting with my back to the window and the sun was beaming on my back making my back really hot. So I asked my son, "Is your back hot son?", and he responded, "No." I started sweating and I thought I wanted to take my shirt off it was so warm. I could feel Keisha saying, "So, I have your attention now, huh?".

Keisha told me that she wanted me to video tape the sunset, so I kind of rushed my family out of the restaurant because the sun was starting to set and there's a very small window. As I was driving away from the restaurant, we were driving up a hill that gave me an excellent view of the sunset. I thought to myself, "I would get a better view if I were across the street but there was oncoming traffic and I couldn't figure out how to make it happen. Then, I heard Keisha's voice saying, "I'll make it happen", and the next thing you know, the stop light turned red and I was able to jump out and catch the photos that I needed. What was so beautiful is that at a certain angle, I could see the telephone poles on the skyline, but in the picture, it looked as if they were three crosses lined up next to each other, suspended in the air, and the sunlight was the backdrop. The picture was amazing! This was one of the most beautiful sunsets I had ever witnessed! I took several more pictures, not really knowing how they would turn out. Afterwards, as my family stood there amaze at the shots I had just captured, I started filming what was in front of me. I kept filming until my camera stopped.

Her Presence

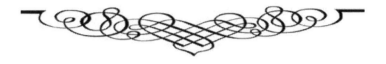

I once read somewhere that the spirit leaves the body very quickly after the death under normal circumstances, but when a death is traumatic, the spirit may linger in limbo between the physical and the spiritual realm. I don't believe that Keisha experienced any pain in her transition, but I do believe she watched herself go through the transition as her spirit was leaving her body and I believe that she was already at peace. I believe that it was because of the bond we shared, that my spirit was open to communicate with her in the hospital. Based on our experience in Heaven, I believe that she was given a choice to remain here in the physical realm until she was buried to comfort me and my family. My Mother even commented that she often felt Keisha's presence like when my mother went to check the van out before buying it and several times when she rode in the van.

We all would feel Keisha's presence on occasion. My mother remembered that she even felt Keisha open doors for her at times. I remember my other sister saying that her clock stopped at the same time that she used to pick Keisha up in the morning. It was amazing to me that one day, I noticed that one of my watches stopped at 7:23, as a matter of fact, ALL of my watches stopped on the same day and it tripped me out! There was another day I remember I was in my kitchen playing a CD that I had made with Keisha in mind, and it felt like Keisha was dancing on my feet again as if she was 5 years old. I thought to myself that it was as if she didn't know she had died yet.

Keisha shared with me at some point that she saw herself motionless in the hospital and that when the doctors pronounced her dead, she thought, "What do you mean I'm dead? I'm not dead! I can see my family! I spoke to my Big Brother! He can see and talk to me." I didn't want to believe that she had died either. We all didn't want to believe it. I had to tell her that it was true. I didn't realize that it would be so painful to tell a loved one that they've died. To see that loved one in the spirit realm is amazing. I still hear my little sister's voice to this day.

I had been through so much that it was overwhelming to me and I felt that God wanted to show me more, but that would require me to have a deeper relationship with Him. So, I made a decision to turn my life over to Christ and on March 17, 2009, I was baptized at First Baptist Church of Glenarden where I fellowship to this day. I wanted my soul to be cleansed. It felt good starting over and going back to church to strengthen my relationship with God. I would sit there during the ceremony thinking, I really want to be closer to my little sister's spirit. I want to go to heaven again, this time being baptized because I really felt that I would see things through a different lens, one that was rooted in my connection with God.

I remember it was a Tuesday. In preparation for the ceremony, men are advised to wear a plain white t-shirt. When you arrive, you are provided with the appropriate clothing to wear during the ceremony, and I remember all of it feeling very sacred. Before the ceremony started the first prayer was given by Reverend Simms. As I closed my eyes to pray, I started seeing sparkles. So, I opened my eyes for a moment, just to make sure the room I was in didn't have any weird lighting issues going on. I closed my eyes again and the sparkles came back. The sparkles were brilliant and they burst into a million stars. I could hear my little sister's voice, "Hey, Big Brother!". I started to cry because I was so emotional. She said, "Don't start crying! I'm happy for you!"

I was thinking about Keisha and I thought to myself, "I miss you, Keisha. I love you so much! I'm sorry for crying, I'm just happy to see you." I replied. "Can you look at me?" she asked. I did so lifting my head up, but leaving my eyes closed. "This is your day, Big Brother. I'm so happy for you! I'll see you later, Big Brother."

I opened my eyes and walked to the platform to talk to Reverend Berkley. They asked me to give my name and as the Reverend recited the instructions, I walked into the water, and then whoosh! Reverend Berkley placed me down into the water. As the Reverend placed me under the water, I could see my little sister hovering over me. When the Reverend brought me back up out of the water, I felt so refreshed. I wanted to tell everyone present, "I love you! Thank you all!" I wondered if they could see what I'd seen. I felt anew knowing that Jesus died for me, covering my sins, and then rose from the dead. I believe that! I renewed my vow to Christ right then and there on March 17, 2009!

Questions People Ask Me

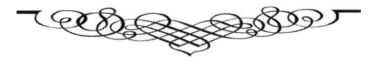

I get asked lots of questions like: "How did you feel going to heaven?"

My answer is, "Extraordinary! To go to paradise, it was magnificent to see and be a part of that experience." God allowed me to go to heaven without crossing over yet. I felt really loved. I realize that there aren't many people living who have experienced heaven as I did. I enjoyed every minute of heaven. All of the angels and butterflies transforming into angels was my favorite part but, there are no words in any language that I could use to really describe how I felt.

"What was it like to see your sister right after her death?"

My answer is, "When I saw her in the hospital, she told me not to be afraid but I was nervous and emotional, and it took her to tell me to calm down because too much emotion would impact my ability to focus on the spiritual experience. It was very calming really. My sister reminded me of when we were younger and used to talk about what it would be like to go to heaven so this experience was like getting a Big Brother award.

Another popular question is, "What are angels like?"

My answer is, "I specifically remember that they smell like sugar cookies and that they speak in harmony. When I first got to heaven, it was like my little sister had angels who were assigned to her and I was hoping I would have angels assigned specifically to me too. When I first saw my angel, we made eye contact, and I could feel that the connection was "special." I felt the purest love, without any other communication. I looked over to my little sister and she said, "Man, Big Brother, the angel is beautiful and it's looking at you!". It's was astounding to me to think I could feel love from someone that quickly. That was something that I distinctly remember is that feeling and expressing love in heaven is completely different than the way we feel and express it in the physical realm.

What is the Book of Life?

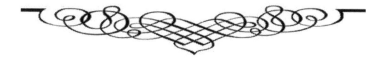

My answer is, "If you stood in front of a fifty-foot-long by twelve-foot-high flat screen, that's how the book of life looks. Very flat! While being weightless, I tried to touch it, but it moved back. When my little sister stood in front of it, it moved forward to touch her. I remember saying, "It's a TV, Keisha! What else could it be?" I didn't have a clue at that time it was a "book." When she touched it and it was like it came on, and it left me speechless. I couldn't move! When it started flashing, at first I couldn't see anything except white flashes. When I started believing it was a book, the flashing started to slow down into and I started to see pictures that reflected memories of when my little sister was a child all the way up to her passing. It was like standing in front of a movie screen. We enjoyed it, we were laughing and smiling the whole time while watching my little sister's life flash before us."

How do you feel about experiencing heaven?

My answer is, "There are no words to describe how I feel, maybe special, that God let me experience heaven with my little sister. Today I have so much love for everyone and, I give that love freely. My heart goes out for those who are in need of love. I wish I could help everyone feel love. It felt like my spirit was so filled with happiness, joy, and love and I had an overwhelming desire to share it with everyone around me. After returning from heaven, the experience gave me a greater sense of belief in myself and though I have always had confidence and belief in myself and tried to apply that to everything I try to do, with- out doubt, the feeling was even more intense now. I felt even more passionately about encouraging everyone to first believe in themselves before expecting anyone else to believe in you. Faith is so key to your belief, so you simply must have faith. I always do. No, I'm not perfect but, I continue to strive higher, to get closer to it."

How did you get your spiritual abilities?

My answer is, "I have always felt that I had spiritual gifts and abilities very early in life. At first, when I was younger, I didn't understand that what I was experiencing were spiritual gifts. It took the death of my little sister to open my spiritual eyes and understanding about it all. Through the years, my gifts have developed and matured into something special. I know now, in hindsight, that the purpose for my journey to heaven was specifically to return and share about my experience and how it has altered my life. I've always been in denial about my gifts and I always knew that sharing my experiences of seeing and listening to angels would gain me nothing but ridicule and humiliation from my peers. It's funny now that I look back because sometimes I'd wear sunglasses just so I can see the aura around a person and with the glasses I could stare without consequence.

How did it feel to have an out of body experience?

My answer is, "It felt surreal, even unbelievable. I didn't recognize myself though I could see a man sitting at a table. It wasn't like looking in the mirror, it was like watching someone else only I knew it was me. It was pretty amazing, feeling weightless, feeling what it felt like to fly.

I would experience flying in my dreams when I was younger and I feel like God was using those dreams to prepare me for the out of body experience.

What other gifts and abilities to you have?

My answer is, "I've also been given the gift of discernment, which is the ability to have an instinctual insight, empathy, or sensitivity to what other's might be thinking or feeling in a way that the average person might not otherwise be aware of. When it's all said and done, I just want to express the overwhelming gift of my kindness and gratitude, and use my spiritual gifts to enlighten the world with the divine awareness of God's love."

Trying To Move On

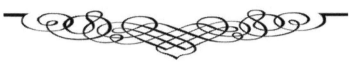

The day after my little sister was buried, the family had the task of going through Keisha's belongings, but it was very difficult for us and for a lot of our other family and friends who lost Keisha to try to move on. We had to go over to her house and remove everything, and I was concerned that at that time I was so sensitive that I felt like if I touch something of her's, I could see her using it. So, though going to her house was special to me, it was equally as painful.

My dad was especially having a hard time with the move. Luckily, there wasn't much that had to be moved. My dad got to Keisha's house first with my brother O'Shea. Keisha's daughter's father was there as well. My mother took most of Keisha's belongings and her generous heart told her to give the bulk of Keisha's things away to people in need. My mother was trying to move on, but this was especially hard because this was her baby.

My sister Ty was having a hard time as well. She and Keisha worked together, riding to work together every day was their normal routine. Now her ride to work would be different.

They used to send each other e-mails at least once a day. Now Ty was left with old e-mails. How do you move on? How do I move on?

As I was driving back to my house, I had so much on my mind, I didn't know where to start. I started writing down everything I experienced on paper because it became so overwhelming. I really didn't know how to move on. Some days I would cry so hard that I'd just go to sleep afterwards, hoping that when I got up everything I was feeling would all be just a bad dream. I would call Keisha's phone just to hear her voice, knowing that she wasn't going to pick up, and sometimes, I would call back to back because it was the closest I could get to her. I was really in denial that my little sister had died. Not my little sister! Not my Keisha! When you lose a friend, you still cry, and you're saddened for their family, but just think what they're going through. That's what I'm going through losing a loved one. It really broke my heart. I never spoke to a therapist about my experience of losing my little sister, however, I have spoken to my parents and Ty about it. Their love is what helped me to focus so I could remember this heavenly event. We all were changed by my little sister's death, however we're more spiritually connected now more than ever before.

My little sister's death had broken all of our hearts, but I knew that joy would eventually come back to all of us. All I could feel was hope from my experience in heaven. It was as if Keisha's passing was the mechanism that triggered us all to start expressing our love toward each other even more, only this time, we were expressing it with all of our hearts. Love was in the air and the fact of the matter is that we needed it. I started noticing that there were more family gatherings planned and though it felt weird not having my little sister there it was still a blessing for all of us to be together. I knew that even though she wasn't there physically anymore, she was still with us in all of our hearts. It was difficult knowing that Keisha wouldn't be there as we each walked through the door. "Hello, everybody," she used to say with a smile! That wouldn't happen anymore. Now we only have great memories. I could hear her even now if I closed my eyes, and I could even imagine seeing her. Her love makes me just feel better both inside and out.

I also remember when Keisha spent a day with Dad, and she was dancing and laughing with him at my parent's house. She had called me Tuesday to ask me this crazy question, "Is Goofy a dog or a walrus? I'll bet you a dollar he's a walrus." She called me back in a minute, laughing, "I owe you a dollar, Big Brother!"

I remember telling a friend that I had a bad feeling about Keisha. I'm not sure if I was having a premonition or not. I wonder sometimes if I knew she was going to die? I was certainly feeling like something was off or like something bad was going to happen, but honestly, I didn't want to think about it. I don't know how or why I felt that feeling or how I could tell how I knew, but I just know I felt a sinking feeling in my spirit. The thought was heavy and it actually made me cry day and night. I remember wanting to get to the bottom of it so I would call Keisha and ask her, "How do you feel?", "Good," she answered. I asked her, "Are you depressed?", "No," she responded. It was as if God was telling me something, but I couldn't make sense of. I should've gone to see her in person.

I was very proud about the fact that my little sister had actually written a book called "Who I Am". It had just came out months before her death. She had the same gift as me and it was so ironic that she was experiencing the same challenges that I had, trying to explain what it was like to experience discernment, for instance, and it was difficult to share with others because people in general had a difficult time understanding the gift itself, not to mention the frustration associated with that. She always helped others get their lives in order. She had an out-of-body experience as well. Who could she tell this to? Who would listen to her? Would you think she was crazy? Most people would say yes! But, I didn't because I was having those experiences too. If you have an out-of-body experience, you should tell someone that you are close to and trust so that you don't feel like you are alone. God has allowed you to have these experiences.

My little sister expressed to me how alone she felt before sharing her experiences with me. The whole decision not to tell anyone was based on her not wanting to be different, so she would express herself by writing it in her book. What I know now won't bring her back, but my hope is that I can now help someone who might be going through what we've been through.

This is a wonderful opportunity to help others see the good in their gifts and in their lives. My little sister is an angel and always will be. Keisha's experiences with her gifts and the frustration of not being able to share with anyone where really overwhelming to her. It mirrored what my experiences were with my gift and the frustration of not having anyone to share it with, but I'm sharing them with you. She didn't. She just kept to herself.

The week before she passed away, every time we spoke I could feel her energy coming toward me and then moving away from me. It overwhelmed me. I kept asking her over and over if she was okay because I still had this sinking feeling in my spirit and every time she would reply, "Yes! What's wrong with you?" I just couldn't explain the feeling I was having about her then. I blamed myself every day after her passing for her death. That's why I took it so hard. The first time she visited me I apologized because I kept feeling like it was my fault, but she would reply, "Big Brother, it's not your fault. Don't blame yourself." She knew I was feeling bad like it was my fault and that I took her death very hard.

I waited so long to get this book published because it was so difficult to swallow the reality that Keisha was gone, that we shared the experience of heaven, and just all that happened to me during that time. It took me a long time to understand that I don't have to share or defend my experience. It simply was what it was. It happened, and I've been touched by God's love. I had an angel walk through me and it changed me, but most of all, God allowed me to experience heaven all day with my little sister.

I'm crying now as I'm sharing this with you because I'm so thankful and joyful that you get to share my extraordinary heavenly experience. I'm so honored to share this event, I've put my heart and soul into this book. I pray that you feel all of the love and tears of joy on every page. I've cried on every page. I might cry when I meet you. I am here. I am alive, walking and talking because of God's love. Heaven is so beautiful and peaceful and I will always have the memory of the experience, with every blink I take, I can visit heaven. God has blessed me with some extraordinary gifts. If you ever experience something like a visit to heaven, you will see many angels there and if you ever need them, all you have to do is call on them. You may not see them in the physical sense, but they will come, they are real, and their love is so pure. I've felt their love and I was touched by an angel.

Dad

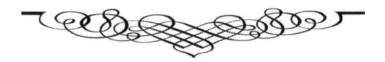

I really want to talk about my Dad because I believe that the gifts both Keisha and I had were passed down from my Dad. As I reflect back on my childhood, I realize that my dad also had gifts of the spirit and I can't imagine how difficult it may have been for him growing up without anyone to share his experiences with might have been for him.

I always felt like my Dad was the coolest man in the world. My Dad has always been very calm and patient and he was blessed to be born a very handsome man. My Dad has green eyes, light skin, wavy hair, personality, and charm. My dad became a father when he was seventeen. At the time he was a basketball star in high school with dreams of becoming a professional basketball player, but that path was altered due to my birth. Dad finished high school at Northwestern Senior High in Hyattsville, Maryland. He started working, but still had love for the game. Unlike me, my dad didn't have a father growing up as a kid, however he did have other men around him to guide him in the right direction. Being a dad was hard for him mentally because he was so very young, but he didn't give up at it, he never gave up and in spite of his lack of parenting skills he always encouraged us to be better than him. Because my Dad was so young, it did make things harder for my mother because the parenting responsibilities did mostly fall on her and she was equally as young and inexperienced at parenting as he was.

As I got older, I started looking at my dad differently. As the years passed, I was learning from him in every way at every moment possible, it was important to me that I learn how to mimic everything positive about him and I wanted to be just like my Dad. My Dad was also very talented and could draw very well. He just never pursued it like he did basketball. My dad is very creative, so I know I got those skills directly from his side of the family. I can remember, at age five, he would have me stare at a specific area on the wall for a few minutes. He said, "What did you see when you focused on that specific area?" Dad was trying to see if I also had a creative eye. I replied, "A star." He burst into laughter. He said, "You're right! To someone else it's just a spot, but to you and I, it's a star!" That was the beginning of my discovering my own creative eye. It had significant impact on how I would look at everything for the rest of my life. Even in the simple things like trees, clouds, and even water I would search for patterns that would resemble something else.

My dad and I would go outside and look at everything, trying to see what else we could see in it. My mother disliked how he had me looking at things in the world differently. She said, "Stop doing that because people are going to think he's crazy!", but I look back now and I am really grateful that my Dad challenged me to learn to look at things differently. It has taught me to seek out the beauty of things, no matter what it is.

I just want to give a special thanks to my dad because I feel that I am so in tuned with my creativity because of his encouragement and support when I was becoming a teenager that I really started coming into my gift of creativity.

I also remember my dad telling me once that he had an experience seeing a ghost or a spirit when he was young and this was the first time I realized that my dad also had spiritual experiences, but he too was in denial about it. He told me that he saw this spirit standing in the doorway as he played with his toys. What do you say when your dad tells you something like that? Honestly, as a kid I always thought that my both of parents were invincible and that they weren't scared of anything at any time. Dad went on to tell me that he wasn't afraid of it, he was just watching it walk past the doorway and then it faded out. It was comforting to know that if my Dad wasn't scared, then there was no reason for me to be scared. It was also comforting to know that I wasn't alone in having experienced something like that. I asked him why he hadn't told us about his experiences sooner and he just said, "Your Mom didn't want me to scare you guys or have you thinking about those kind of things" so he always kept it to himself, at least until Mom wasn't around. Then he would share a story or two with us. I guess he was checking to see if any of us had experienced anything like that. I wanted to tell him so badly that I had similar experiences, but I was scared because I always knew my parents thought I was "special". I did share with my sisters though because when we would see or experience something strange I would be spooked!!!

I've told my dad I love him and thanked him for bringing me into this world because he is who he is, which made me a well-rounded person. I want to believe that I make him proud of me for writing this book. It's because of my dad that I am who I am.

My dad would spend time with us when he wasn't working. My dad is the creative one. This is where I perfected a trait that he taught my sister and I. My dad would have us stare at an object such as clouds, trees, you name it. Then he used to say, "You have to be creative and use a creative eye and mind. If you develop this trait, you have to perfect it. Doing this will make you see things other people can't see." My dad was very creative with art, handwriting, and painting. He was in my life every hour, every day, doing something creative. He would have you look at something, for example, a cloud, and tell him what you see. He could see it. We really couldn't see anything until we focused. Once you focused, you could see everything and anything. My mother would tell him, "You'll make those kids seem crazy to others," she would sometimes shout! "Stop doing that!" So, he stopped. We would tell him what we saw at times and he would look without saying a word. He would nod his head up if we were right, or down if we were wrong. His creativeness made me strive harder to see what he saw, only quicker. With a blink of an eye I became better. I wanted to be perfect at doing this. I wanted to be "a perfectionist" at everything my dad would teach or show me, from creative art or images, to everything I do. I wanted to perfect it. With my skills so on point, I became better at what he showed me.

Mother

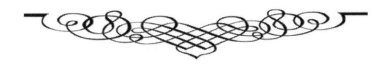

I also want to take some time to talk about my Mom. When I was a child, I thought my mother was the prettiest lady in the world! Mom always had a smile on her face, she always smelled lovely she had this unique scent like a "roses straight from heaven." She must have used that scent to make my dad fall in love with her! The two of them fell for each other, having me nine months later. When I was born, my mother said I was special. My mother attended Blair Northwestern High School, having me when she was fifteen years old, It was so hard for her because during this time, while her friends were all partying, she was at home taking care of a child.

I remembered this incident like it happened only a minute ago. When I was three years old, I walked out of the house, I grabbed my toy, a yellow, steel truck, I crossed the street, walked up a steep hill and I got on top of this toy truck and rode down the hill at top speed – probably at 10 miles per hour. No brakes! I laughed the whole ride down the hill! My mother never understood why or how I never got hurt or injured when I did that because there was traffic both ways because the street is in a T-pattern! I shocked my mom and dad all the time with the fact that I was so young and just didn't have any fear!

Since I was three years old, I have always had a fascination with animals, particularly the ones around my house. I always felt a bond with the squirrels and birds because I would always feed them and in my mind, I felt as though they were all my buddies. I can also remember when I would climb out of the window to feed the squirrels on the top of the roof right on the ledge, sometimes standing on the gutters with my arms out like I was flying! I used to enjoy that so much! I sometimes can still feel it. My mother and I recently talk about those days and just laughed! I love seeing her laugh. I used to do things to purposefully make her laugh really hard!

You know, the kind of laughter that makes you choke and puts tears in your eyes. My mother is a very smart lady and very good with her hands. She always told me never say, "I can't", but instead said that I should always try. She would encourage me and tell me, "Don't give up". I actually learned how to tint windows from my mother. Even though when she did it and it didn't come out smoothly, she never stopped trying to teach me. She even learned how to caulk around the windows in our house. It looked like cake frosting, but guess what? She always tried. I believe that it was my mother that made me become a perfectionist. My grandmother, Lorraine Delaney, or "Mama", as we so endearingly called her, who was a beautiful lady, who would care for my sister and I when my parents would be in school or at work. There wasn't anything we couldn't have to eat. There was nothing she couldn't make, either! I remember she would kiss me so many times. She sat me on her lap and said, "You are a special person. Always show love for others who are so in need. I love you so much." It was kind of hard being the special one, especially when there are other kids living in the house, but I was her "Special One." I've done so many incredible things in my life, I figure I had to be born with this luck! I really felt like I was the luckiest kid in the world. Even my Uncle Darryl would always tell me how lucky I was, even up to this day.

I've never told anyone this before, this is the first time. I remember there was a time that I stood in front of my grandmother, and I remember her saying, "I can't breathe! I can't breathe!" I stood there with tears in my eyes, hoping this was a joke. It wasn't! Everyone was panicking! I stopped crying, watching my "mother" hold her chest in such pain. She looked at me. I will NEVER forget that look. With tears in her eyes, I could feel her love deep within. Moments later my grandmother would be taken to the hospital. That was the last time I saw her rocking in her red chair. She passed away that evening. No matter what I did, she would always say, "I love you. You are special. Don't let anyone tell you differently".

I remember seeing this glow around my grandmother. The same glow that I saw around my friend that I used to play games with when I was a child, and I remember seeing the same glow around his mother, and my little sister. That explains why my sister and my family thought I was talking to myself all the time, but I wasn't. I could see the kid and the mother all the time.

Every time I went outside to play. He was there with the angels. Now, in hindsight, I realize that when we are children, we tend to be able to see these things a lot more than when we become adults.

Days passed by and I remember asking my Auntie Flo, "Where's Ma at?" She replied, "Ma is in heaven." I asked, "Where is that?" With tears in her eyes, she explained, "Look outside in the sky." I looked with tears in my eyes. My tears were from confusion, not knowing what heaven was and feeling sad that Momma was now somewhere far away where I couldn't see her anymore. All I knew is that heaven had my grandmother, and everyone was crying. I'm crying as I write this because the love she had for me was so pure that nothing in my life can ever compare. She saw something in me at an early age. I can't forget how she used to tell me I was special. I was young, but I could feel her love. To feel love like that was astounding to me. I'm not saying my mother's love isn't pure. My grandmother would look me eye-to-eye with love in her eyes, her heart, and her touch, and I truly miss her. The glow my Ma had was so amazing, but no one said that they saw it around her. So, how could I see it? Maybe that's why our love was a such a special love. Her eyes were so wonderful. I could see myself in them. I always loved looking at her.

I love you so much Momma, and I wish you could see me now walking out my life. I can hear you in the spirit realm. I feel your love deep within me.

Due to my grandmother's passing, my mother took on more responsibilities. We stayed there at the house for another two years and my parents moved from Takoma Park to Hyattsville. I was now five or six years old. My mother and father spent long hours at work. My sister and I had clothes and toys, but were missing that grandmother love. My mother's sister, Auntie Flo came over to care for us while mom and dad worked. We had so much fun with Auntie. I grew closer to Auntie because she looked more like my grandmother than all of them. There was that love I so adored. Every time she would leave, I would cry so much. I'd cry myself to sleep. I had my sister there to comfort me at times. The thought of my grandmother leaving me was so heartbreaking to me. I never recovered from her death. To be attached to my auntie at times became hard for my mother, because it might have made her feel like she was in second place in my heart. I started hanging with my mother more often and the love I had for my mother was growing deeper. I could feel my grandmother's love through my mother now.

    I never told her this before, but I wish I could hear my Mother's laughter all the time. My mother, sister and I would race from the car to the house, and my mother would always let us win! She had this laugh that was contagious and it would make you laugh every time you hear it.

    I loved her laugh so much. I told my sister that I would do anything for her. We shared so much together. We were raised like twins, always dressing alike. Always! As we got older, you couldn't break us apart. We were one! One heartbeat.

My Grandmother

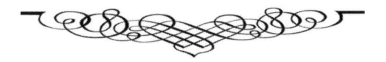

My dad's mother, Catharine Clark, was a very spiritual lady. I loved her dearly. A grandmother's love is always different. She would give me things my mother wouldn't. It was all love. I remember her telling me I was special and I wasn't like other kids. I didn't know what she meant by that as a kid, but once I grew up and came into my teenage years, I knew what she was talking about. I would talk to her about my dreams and how I could fly in my dreams. I would help people in my dreams get out of trouble or danger. She really enjoyed me telling her about my dreams until one day I told her I dreamt of people who had died.

Those people who had died in my dreams were lost and needed help. I would listen to them talk and sometimes laugh. She never once said I was crazy or just making this up because it was too vivid in detail. I used to see this gold glow around people who were near death. I tried blocking this out of my mind because it was too hard for me to fathom that it meant they were close to death. As I got older, I blocked a lot of things out of my mind, specifically things that I knew were maybe implied death, or the visions that I would get when I would meet someone and I could see about experiences they may have had that caused them pain, as if I could see their sadness, but no matter how hard I tried, it came back again. There was a time I told my Granny about these things and I remember her saying that I was her special grandson and that one day I would know why. That day wouldn't come soon enough for me. As she lay in the hospital bed, very sick, she would ask me, "Do you see that glow around me?" and I started crying because I could, but she said it was okay "It will just be our secret".

After my grandmother died, I would hear my grandmother's voice sometimes and it would give me chills, and then I would feel this warm breeze. I've never told anyone until now because I didn't want to sound weird or have people look at me like I was crazy, but now I feel comfortable talking about it be- cause there are 18 years between her passing to where my life is now. My grandmother and I shared so many things and now, in hindsight, I look back and can finally understand what some of those things meant. My grandmother was the first person to say that God gave me special eyes and talents, but at the time, I didn't understand that they were gifts and abilities, but she explained to me that having empathic abilities, or a spirit of discernment, or having visions of past, present, and future events were all special gifts from God.

I used to absolutely LOVE going to my grandmother's house. It's funny now that I look back because my parents would send me over to grandmother's house as a part of being disciplined, and sometimes, I would act up on purpose just so I could get sent over to my Grandmother's house cause I knew there was a candy bar waiting for me!!! Little did they know I used to LOVE IT! I always knew that going over to Grandmother's house would mean that I would have all of my Grandmother's attention all to myself, I would get to freely express myself, and I would get to eat all of my favorite things. We would have fresh fried fish, chicken, and pork chops, greens, squash, because she had a garden where she grew a lot of things and they always tasted better for some reason because she cooked it! I also loved that I knew every time that I went to Granny's house, I would get to go the store for her which meant that she would always give me enough to get some special treats for me like my favorite candy bars, or a bag of chips and a soda. I would also look forward to seeing my Uncle Cel (which was short for Marcel) because he lived with Granny. I now understand that she knew me better than I knew myself at the time since I was so little. I am grateful for everything she gave of herself to me because she has contributed greatly to who I am today. I miss her today and I always will.

A Star

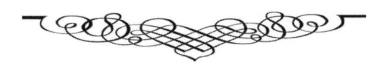

I've always believed that I was blessed with special gifts that only God could have placed in me. I also believe that God is the only one who could unlock these gifts in me when they were supposed to come to life because He is the source of everything. When I was little, I remember telling my parents that "I chose them" to be my parents and I remember the look on both of their faces of utter amazement! I've overheard my Mom saying to my Dad, "Why does he keep saying that to us? What makes him say that?" and my Dad responding with, "He's a unique kid!". In fact, it's my belief that I could see my parents from heaven through the stars and that I chose them to be my parents before I was even conceived.

Going back to one Friday night in 1968, the sky was so clear that it looked as if you could touch every star in the sky. The moon was full and I remember looking down from heaven at my parents. As they looked up in the sky they always noticed one star in particular. This wasn't just any star, this was a star that represented their love and it seemed that it followed them everywhere and they were always able to find it whenever they looked at the stars together. Every time they looked at the stars together it made them love each other more. They used to spend time looking at the stars whenever they could, even naming the ones that they knew, but one of the brightest stars was their favorite and I have always felt like that star might have been a window from heaven that allowed me to see them before I was born, almost as if I was communicating with them before I was conceived. It was as if I was trying to let them know I was coming so I would send them love whenever they looked up at that star. They felt love come over their souls. My parents never told me this story. I always felt that I knew about the star in the sky being special to them and that it represented their love even though they had never mentioned it to me. My parents had no idea that star would affect their lives forever.

Later on my parents went looking back up in the sky for that one bright star, but it wasn't there anymore, it was as if it had vanished. One night they were looking for it but couldn't find it and they looked at each other in disbelief, my parents were amazed, puzzled, and sad. As that night wet on, my mother mentioned that she felt different. She had this feeling come over her that she couldn't put into words. As she tried to express it to my father didn't know how to console her, all he could do was hold her. As they held each other as they looked up at the sky again, only this time their star of love appeared to them. This time, their star was even brighter than ever and this time my mother touched her stomach and realized that she was pregnant. I believe that it was in that moment that she and I both knew that God would bless me to be a gift to my parents and that there was a special purpose that I as conceived into the universe.

I've always thought that I was made specifically from a touch of God's heavenly light and love. I chose my parents to gain their experiences and at the same time change the way they love one another. I wanted to show them my way of loving someone deep within in an effort to help them learn to push away their negativity. My instincts and intuitive senses have been with me since I was born. I displayed an unusual set of psychological attributes that parents, teachers, and doctors couldn't explain at the time. I knew that I was going to be unique.

Growing up, I was misunderstood all the time by my parents and others. I had special events in my life that couldn't be explained. I wanted to let my parents know before I was even born what to expect. I tried to communicate to them before I was even born to warn them that I wouldn't speak much because my thoughts would come at me so fast and I actually didn't speak until I was five, but I would communicate with them telepathically. I was a phenomenal child with multiple talents. Only my parents had to believe what they saw with their own eyes, but couldn't always explain. I wanted to tell them not to treat me differently, not to worry about what people and family would say about me, not to be in denial of what they might see me do, and not to try and manipulate me or lie to me because I will know when they did. I would notice any hidden agendas from anyone trying to hide something from me. I would see people and things spiritually that others wouldn't see. To feel love would be very important to me, so I wanted them to always tell me that they love me, no matter what. My intelligence and wisdom would be far greater than other kids my age. I wanted them to understand that if they allowed their negative energy to smother my energy, they would be unaware of my gifts. In the future, I would visit heaven only to come back again, as a totally different being. My mission here in the physical realm would be to help people who have a hard time after their loved one has crossed over. I've been sent to the physical realm to teach my parents and others about spiritual truths. I would be able to read your emotions, even if you might try to hide them. I'd be very sensitive and detached from most people. I just needed them to honor the Holy Spirit within me and be content with knowing that only love matters in the world.

Saved By An Angel

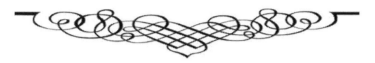

One night, as we left my Grandmother's house, my parents, Ty, and I were riding in my mother's '64 Chevy Impala. We drove up to the "4400 Club," a local club in North Brentwood. My parents asked for two sodas and a bag of chips. Normally, this club was busy, cars going up and down, but for some reason, it wasn't that busy when we pulled up to the drive-thru window. For some reason, I wanted to know if I was strong enough to hold the door, so I thought I would try it. Then I noticed a flash of light by my door. I tried to put my window down, but it was broken. That flash of light was trying to tell me something. This flash of light looked like it had a face. I was so fascinated by this face, but I was so focused on seeing if I was strong enough to hold the door, so I opened the door, while my parents were pulling off. I didn't want to say anything, so I tried to hold onto the door. I noticed the flash followed us. We made a u turn, then out swung the door, and out swung me right out of the car! When we turned the corner my door swung open, causing me to fall out and tumble over and over. "Aaaaaaaaah!" my mother yelled! "Go get him, Louis!" Oh my God! Go get him!" my mother yelled over and over again. My mother and sister started crying. My Dad rushed to stop the car, he put the hazard lights on, and then jumped out of the car to get me and quickly put me back into the car. I could hear my mother yelling, "Hurry up and get him! Oh my God! Are you okay, sweetie? Talk to me!". "I'm okay, Ma," I'm okay."

"No, you're not, baby! You can't be! You tumbled like fifty feet." I can still see the shock and confusion on my parents' faces. Still in shock, my mother rushed me in the house. "Okay, Baby, I know you're hurt," she said, holding her face with both hands, "Please tell me where you're hurt at. How come you're not bleeding? How come he's not bleeding, Louis? He should be bleeding! He doesn't have any scratches on him!". My mother was frantic and she was in complete disbelief.

This is impossible! I remember looking at my parents and my sister's faces. They were amazed! "You scared us so bad. Thank God there were no cars coming down the street, they would've drove right over top of you!" I tried to tell them what happened, but they kept talking over me.

My mother told her sister and the whole family knew. My dad told his mother and sister. The whole town knew what happened to me. What they didn't know is that I saw an angel come from the side of the car when I was sitting in the car, he looked me right in the face and covered me so I wouldn't get hurt. I saw this bright orange light. It happened so fast that my dad didn't notice I was pointing to the angel. Even when I was three years old, the angel that was out there on the ledge with me was the same angel who saved me from this accident that day.

No one ever knew that it was an angel that saved my life until now. I can talk about this event now, but back then who could I have talked to? Who would have believed me? I mostly stayed to myself afterwards, which made me grow even shyer.

Frisbee

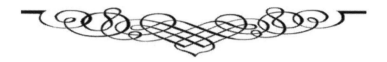

I remember sitting in the living room watching my neighbor play with a frisbee, throwing it up in the air and catching it. Man! Wow! That looks like fun! So I asked my Auntie Flo if I could go outside and play with him. She said I could, so I ran outside. "Hey what's your name," I asked. "Brian," he said. "Show me how you do that. That looks like so much fun!" He called me by my name, and told me to catch the frisbee. "How do you know my name?" I asked. "Oh, your sister told me." I didn't think about it much so I said, "Well, let's finish playing, Brian,". He showed me so many tricks with this frisbee. One day he threw it up in the air so high, it looked like a bird! Wow! What was amazing to me was that I never saw him catch it. It was in his hands before I blinked. He would do this trick every time I saw him. Brian was around eight or nine years old. I was like seven or eight. Brian would knock on the patio doors for me. Tap! Tap! Tap! He would usually come around the same time every day. Some days I couldn't go outside so I had to watch him from inside my house.

My dad watched me do all these frisbee tricks and was

really impressed. He would just walk away from the patio doors, shaking his head. He didn't realize that I was out there playing with Brian, because he couldn't see Brian. I'd ask, "Can I go outside, Daddy?", to which he'd respond, "Yeah, take your sister, too,". I really didn't want my sister playing with us, but since she already told Brian my name, she must have played with his sister before. His sister was seven, but she and I never played together. We came outside and I ran down the grassy field so I could catch the frisbee from Brian. He threw the frisbee down the grassy field toward me, but this time the frisbee slowed down so I could see it spinning, then whoosh! The frisbee went back to normal speed! With my sister looking on, I had to catch it. Somehow now I know she never saw Brian, but we would play for hours!

"Yes! That was awesome, Brian!" I yelled. "That was awesome! Did you see that?" I asked.

She looked at me but didn't say anything. She kept playing with her dolls. "How did you do that trick, Brian?" I threw the frisbee back to Brian so he could do it again. Whoosh! The same slow trick. "How did you do that, Brian!" I yelled.

"Brian?" my sister asked. "You didn't see that frisbee trick?" I asked. "What frisbee trick? You don't even have a frisbee!" "Brian! Come here, show my sister the frisbee trick," I demanded. "She doesn't believe you can do it again", Brian said." I just wanted him to come closer so that Ty could see him, but it didn't matter because Ty wasn't able to see him.

"Who's Brian?" she asked. "Brian! You told Brian my name!" I yelled. "No, I didn't!" "Sure you did. How would he know my name if you didn't tell him?" I turned around to call for Brian. Brian started walking toward us. "Watch, wait till he shows you this trick," I instructed her. As Brian got closer, something amazing started to happen. Every step Brian took playing with the frisbee, he became transparent. I could look straight through him, causing me to wonder how he'd done that trick with my sister looking on. As he got closer to us, he vanished in midair. "Now, that's a magic trick!" I yelled.

"What magic trick?" she asked. "You saw what he done!" I insisted. "He who? Why are you talking to yourself? I'm telling Daddy because you're scaring me," she said. "Wait! The kid that threw me the frisbee, Brian! I've been playing with him for weeks,". "No! You've been playing outside with yourself for weeks," she insisted.

"You saw me run down the grassy field to catch the frisbee." "What frisbee? You ran down the grassy field and started yelling, 'That's an awesome trick!' But you didn't do no trick. I was looking at you swinging your arms up and down, like you was throwing something," She explained. "Yeah, a frisbee!" "What frisbee? You're scaring me! I'm going back in the house and telling Daddy!". "Don't! I was joking with you! I wasn't talking or playing with no one. I'm sorry," I said. When she went back in the house, I turned around to see if I would see Brian. I did, but he was walking down the hill. If my sister didn't see him, maybe I didn't see him, but I knew I caught that frisbee! I stopped believing what I saw when my sister questioned me about Brian. My spiritual connection with Brian faded, causing him to become transparent. All I knew was that I'd been playing with Brian for weeks. I was very confused, upset and very nervous.

I became very shy and would play by myself; not even playing with my sister. I felt lost and confused not knowing what to do about it. I kept having dreams about Brian, my grandmother, and my first friend. I never knew his name. Maybe Brian was his name? Maybe that was when I was younger. They looked a lot alike. Was that Brian who saved me from falling out of the car? It looked like Brian. I couldn't tell anyone what happened to me because they would think I'm crazy. I kept this secret about Brian to myself until now.

I would keep everything I heard and saw to myself for years. I was in denial, and therefore I believe I blocked my ability, or at least tried to ignore it. I became even more shy. I wasn't talking that much to my family. I really just stayed to myself. I was always close with my sister, Ty, yet I just knew I couldn't tell her everything. I became afraid of the dark because I started hearing voices again. I used to put cotton in my ears so I couldn't hear spirits. I blocked everything out. I was really starting to isolate myself so my Mom mentioned that we might need to get a dog and I think that's because she thought that might help to pull me out of my shell. So one day, my mother brought my sister and me to the pound. I'm not sure if my mother could tell or feel my sadness, but the idea of us getting a dog really did make my heart open back up.

When we walked in the dog pound, it felt like I could feel these dogs' sad energy. Even with their tails wagging, I felt their abuse, their sadness. We came across this beautiful dog. He was a shepherd and husky mix. We picked him, and he came home with us. We named him "Max." We played with him every day. It was me and my sister's duty to care for him. Max really brought happiness in the family but, especially for my sister and me. I felt connected to him spiritually. I used to take him on long walks just talking to him. I really felt like he understood me. You know animals have those incredible senses. I felt like Max could protect me from anything.

At this time, Keisha was four years old, but very smart for her age. Her level of thinking was very impressive and years beyond her age. I remember Keisha and I came home to do our homework and chores. I remember panicking because I couldn't find my keys after we got in the house. I remember looking everywhere in the house, upstairs, downstairs, everywhere but no sign of my keys. I knew I would be in so much trouble if my Mom came home and I had to tell her that I lost my keys, but my mother was coming home soon! Keisha touched me and said, "I'll find them for you. They're still in the door."

I couldn't believe her so I said, "No they're not!" We opened up the door slowly, and there they were! "That wasn't it," she said. "Normally you open the door and take ten steps and put them on the table." I asked, "Why do you count everything?" She said, "I always count! They…" "They who?" I asked. "They tell me numbers all the time. Numbers have meaning. Sometimes I see them." I was getting nervous and scared when she told me this and it sent chills through my whole body. I didn't want her going through what I went through as a kid. I kind of knew what she was trying to say. In hindsight now, I realize that my little sister also had this gift and had likely been communicating with angels from the time she was very young as well.

I remember one time, when I was fourteen, I had a dream that my grandfather Leroy Delaney came to me in a dream. I convinced myself it was a dream. I was sleeping in my bed, and he walked into my room. He said, "Hey, you want to go to the Hot Shoppes with me?" I replied, "Yeah, why not. You're my grandfather, but we should ask Ma first." He said, "No, we don't wanna wake her up, she needs her rest. She has had a hard day." When we walked through the door, I turned into a kid again, a five-year-old kid with his grandfather. I could not stop laughing because I thought it was the coolest magic trick. He said, "Sssssshhh, not so loud. Watch this trick." We floated down the stairs and walked through a metal door. Wow! All I thought was how amazing it was. "How did we do that Dadda?" "Shhhhh, you'll wake your momma," he said.

We got into a 1974 station wagon, the one he always drove. We drove to the bottom of the hill and turned the corner. We then got into a white Chevy pick-up truck with blue seats. We drove to the Hot Shoppes in Takoma Park. This was his favorite restaurant. He said I could get anything I wanted. I noticed a lady with angel eyes looking at me. I felt her touch my soul. She walked up to my grandfather and asked, "Mr. Delaney?", "Yes, Sugar." She couldn't stop looking at me. As I looked around the room, everyone had this gold glow around them. It looked like every- one was standing or sitting in front of the car's headlights. Now I've seen this glow before with my grandmother and friends. I can remember everything I saw before, like what each person was wearing down to the details. For instance the manager had coffee stains on his blue tie, there was a run in one of the waitresses' stockings, the lady's hair net that wouldn't stay intact, or the older Caucasian man who was short on money (literally thirteen cents short). The waitress still gave him his coffee, free. I noticed my granddad, "Dadda" as I used to call him, adjusting his pants with a white patch that read, "Delaney, Leroy" on it. His green pants, brown boots and white t-shirt, green shirt also had a patch with "Leroy" on it. He was wearing a hat and a brown belt. He had one grapefruit with a spoon and one coffee with four sweet-n-low. He asked for more sweet-n-low, with a laugh. He said, "I don't suppose you have that much sugar, but who knows, it's just you and me here, son." He paid for his meal with two dollars and fifty-five cents. I had ice cream, but what was amazing, we didn't eat anything with our mouths! No one did. But I could taste it!

As we returned to the station wagon, I could hear my mother's voice calling me. My granddad asked me not to tell anyone what had happened until the time was right. My mother's voice got louder. I looked at my granddad, and he disappeared right in front of me. I could hear him, "You love your mother and father always, okay? Love you, son." My granddad never told my mother he loved her when she was growing up. I wanted to tell my mother so much that "dada said he loves you and thanks for caring for him when your mother passed away." I kept that secret. I kept that secret for so long. I did tell her I had a dream about her father. I told her I woke up so confused because everything that happened felt so real to be a dream. The colors, everyone happy, joyful and the glow.

She replied, "That was a dream." I knew I had heard my

granddad's voice, but now was not the time to tell her. She wouldn't understand. She wasn't impressed with my dreams. I felt at that moment the hurt from her spirit of talking about her father that made her feel lonely. I could see my mother's eye tearing up. After seeing her eyes tear up, I didn't want to say any more. I didn't want to see my mother hurt. She was crying inside and she was feeling helpless. How was I able to feel her feelings? I didn't know at the time. I couldn't feel anything when my dad came around. I think his presence was somewhat shielding my mother's energy keeping her from feeling anything too intense.

My grandfather came to me so many times after that until I thought I was dreaming. The message I got from his visits was "love!" He showed me that he could love people and that he wasn't an angry old man, like people thought he was. He loved all of his kids. He never told them he loved them, but he told me. The experiences I had with him were wonderful. He kept a picture of all of his children in his wallet. He would show this photo to everyone who would look, especially at the Hot Shoppes.

When my granddad passed away, my mother started spending a lot of time by herself, but my little sister gave my mother the strength to continue to find happiness with my sister by her side all the time. They became one and they did everything together. My little sister was around seven, and Ty and I were seventeen. By that time I was very much into learning who I was in the spirit. I vowed not to tell anyone what I knew about myself, or my thoughts, or how I had to control my thoughts or what I shared. I found myself helping people who needed my help and helping my classmates who didn't believe in themselves. I noticed as I looked in people's eyes, I could feel their pain, which goes along with the saying that the "Eyes are the windows to the soul." I used to avoid eye contact all the time because I could see things about people that I just didn't want to see or feel the energy of that thing that I would see. It would drained my energy and I would come home feeling exhausted and I would just want to sleep when I came home from school. Who could I tell what I was experiencing? I didn't want to believe my little sister had the same gift, but she did. I also noticed that my sister had a glow about her just like what I saw on my granddad. I asked Ty one day, "When you look at Keisha, what do you see? Do you see a glow around her?" and she replied, "I don't see anything." It was then that I knew that it was something only I could see.

My First Out of Body Experience

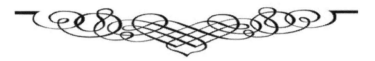

When I was seventeen I was going through so much in my life that my spiritual awareness had risen to a point that everyone I passed in the school hallway I could feel the energy associated with their challenges. Some people I knew lost their parents, aunts, uncles, friends, and teachers. I felt so overwhelmed that sometimes that it felt like my head was going to explode. There were so many hurting souls who were in need of help or relief. People would approach me and start sharing very personal issues with me and it was so random that I never looked at how frequently it occurred. There were times when I felt so heavy with emotion, that it would stress me out and I would need to have some alone time just to clear my head but, living at home didn't always offer time and space for me to do that, so I would walk over to my girlfriend's house because she and her grandmother were spiritual people with good energy and I would feel so much lighter after visiting with them. I knew that I could have ridden my bike or caught the bus but, that would make me encounter too many people and their emotions.

One afternoon at my girlfriend's house, we were sitting on the sofa in the living room and out of the corner of my eye I saw a smoky shadow moving toward us from the hallway. I was in denial about the shadow and tried to play it off like I didn't see it but, then she asked me, "Did you see that?". I said, "Yeah!" We both freaked out a little, looked at each other, and left the apartment. She said later that her grandmother and her saw that shadow in their house all the time, but just blocked it out. I wanted to know more but she refused to talk about it. I didn't know how to express myself back then because I was so shy. I would sometimes see shadows moving around me here and there and they didn't necessarily make me feel scared, as a matter of fact, I often felt like they were there to protect me, so these experiences weren't bad ones, it would just make me feel so disconnected from other people sometimes because I knew that not everyone was having those type of experiences. My girlfriend was sensitive in the same way and would see them too and I believe that's what made us bond during that time in my life. That's why I loved her so much, though sometimes she acted like she didn't see them. I believed she was in denial sometimes too because again, who's gonna believe us and who could we tell that we were having these experiences? Oddly enough, my smell became much more sensitive when I would have these encounters. I could smell my grandfather's aftershave sometimes around our house and it made me feel like he was watching my mother even when I went over my auntie's house.

It didn't matter which aunt or uncle's house, I would smell my granddad's scent sometimes. I could hear his laughter too and all of these encounters were driving me crazy, so I would try to block them out because they were hard for me. I felt so alone! So unloved and I felt scared all the time, knowing that I couldn't tell my parents or my sister Ty, but my little sister Keisha knew because she could tell when I was bothered and she would squeeze my shoulders and tell me that whatever was bothering me, it would be ok. It was so crazy that as young as she was, she was sensitive enough to know that I was going through something difficult and it was so sweet how she would try and comfort me in her own way. She would say, "Do you wanna play Barbie's now?". Little did I know at that time that she understood because she too could see spirits and angels. I could feel what my little sister was feeling. She made me believe that what I saw and heard was normal because she thought it was normal, but she's only seven years old I thought! What did she know about spirits? I asked myself over and over, why me? and how could she? I never got a chance to ask my little sister specifically what she saw and heard as a child. I over-heard her talking to her friend about what she would see and hear. She was in the room playing with her tea set and I heard her say, "Why do you always come play with me when no one's around?" Now, I'm standing in the kitchen behind the refrigerator. "You have to meet my Big Brother, he's funny. You'll love him. All the girls think he's cute, but he's not cute, cuz he's my Big Brother." At first I didn't know what to make of it because I went through the same experience with my friend "Brian." I poked my head around the refrigerator, "Don't go!" she told her friend. I asked her who she was talking to and she gave me this look, like I knew already. She sat there and started to cry. I asked why she was crying. She said, "Because you scared my friend away." I didn't have to ask any more questions! I knew my little sister could see spirits because I had the same look on my face. My little sister became more aware of her surroundings. I was very impressed with her at that age. We started what my dad called, "practicing using our Creative Eye." Just looking at everything: carpets, towels, rocks, paper bags, trees, clouds, water, and so on. We would look at things and see who would come up with a picture first.

Things became fascinating to us. We could see so much more than the naked eye could see. We were so amazed by our abilities. We would ask others what they saw, but what they would see was nothing like how we saw it. My sister Ty also had the creative eye gift too. My little sister could see thing so much faster than all of us. That, to me, was amazing since she was only seven years old.

Later, I found out that my dad had spiritual encounters when he was a child, too. He never said anything to us about it until my little sister died. My dad would be home most of the time but, he and I didn't have a great "father-to-son" relationship at the time. I really didn't think he loved me. I couldn't really talk to him about anything except basketball or boxing, and still, it was like he was in his own world. Now, when we did talk, other topics we talked about where my Dad felt like he could relate was when he would talk with us about using your creative eye.

That's when he seemed to be more engaged with me. Otherwise, and most of the time, I felt pushed away. I truly believe that he experienced something spiritual, or something happened to him that prob- ably scared him and he didn't know how to handle it or express it to anyone at the time. I remember that he tried to tell us this when my sister and I were younger but, we just thought he was just loaded and smoking something. I believe my Dad waited to tell us that he too had similar experiences even though it took him thirty-five years to do it.

There was a point in my life during this period when we didn't see eye-to-eye anymore. I've always loved my dad dearly but, some of the things he chose to do in his life affected the whole family. For that reason, I didn't want to be a part of the family and I wanted to move away. My mother and father never cursed at all. I'm so thankful I never heard curse words from their mouths. I could feel the negative vibes from both my parents. As a teenager I observed a lot of times where my parents didn't speak to each other. I don't know that they understood how these periods of "speechlessness" negatively affected not only me, but our whole family. I used to think that was some reflection of how they felt about me and it hurt me deeply because I felt like they didn't love me. I would think to myself, how do people live together and be completely speechless! They were! This really affected my sister and me. My little sister was too young to understand what was going on.

We all were at odds with each other. This was the time I needed my parents and sister the most. The speechlessness event affected Ty very hard just as it did me. She became shy and distant from my parents and me. I felt so lost not talking to her. We used to talk about everything every day. I felt like every- one was avoiding me. How do you avoid your son, your brother? I didn't feel loved or wanted in the house. I remember going to bed and just crying myself to sleep. I could hear my dad's voice within saying, "Stop crying, boy! Don't cry." But I was crying and it all made me very sensitive since then and even to this day, so I cry easily when events like this happen. It just gets to me. I laid there, crying for a while. Then I got up and walked downstairs. As I opened the door, there was my dog, looking at me. I felt comfort lying there with Max, even though he couldn't talk. I really felt we were communicating back and forth. I cried myself to sleep just holding him all night. So, every time I wanted to cry, I would go sleep with him to comfort me because he would always show me love. He showed me love every day. I really had a special bond with my Max. I used to think that if anything ever happened to Max, I wouldn't know what to do. It felt like he was my only friend in the family during this time. I would take him for long walks and literally talk to him about how I was feeling or what I was going through. Max was my confidant, my therapist, my little buddy and even though he couldn't speak back I felt like he understood me, never judging me, but always listening and affectionate enough to let me know in his own special way that he loved me and that everything would be alright.

    I find that sometimes, when I'm feeling bad or thinking about things in the past, I dream about Max, and some of the other dogs I've had in my life, coming back to visit me and comfort me when I'm going through something. Thinking of Max makes me think of a time when his company offered me a sense of peacefulness that I almost couldn't find during that time in my family's house.

Growing up in the household became very stressful. I felt unloved and unwanted. My mother and I were continually arguing with each other. She would blame me for not living up to her standards, which made me a perfectionist. The tension between my mother and me intensified, and I made up my mind that I couldn't live there anymore. The house became so sad for me. I wanted to take my own life. I really felt I was so alone and un- loved. It came to a point that I didn't want to look anything like my dad. He never told me he loved me. My mother never told us she loved us because she was never told that by her parents. Love is all I wanted, and I wasn't getting it. When I would see visions about people and hear music or instruments in my head it was just starting to be too much for me. I didn't know how to handle it. I just really wanted it to stop! Feeling insignificant and even invisible was more than I could handle and that I didn't even exist, so I thought, I might as well not exist.

That night, I was very upset to the point of tears. I kept asking myself, "who's going to help me now", and I responded to myself, "nobody!". It was at that point that I had made a decision that I didn't want to be alive anymore, so I went downstairs to find some aspirins. As I laid down to go to sleep, I took ten aspirin pills and laid down without planning to wake up the next day. I had a vision about Max coming to me right before I dosed off. In the vision, he could communicate his thoughts to me and that night I dreamed that I was walking my dog and he spoke to me. He said, "If you die, who's going to walk and feed me? I love you. You love me. You got to get up now." I got up, thinking I was dead already. As I was lying there, I could see myself hovering over my body. Seeing this for the first time scared me. I didn't know that was me because I looked different. I walked through my door and my sister's door. I could see her lying there peacefully and so happy. I went downstairs and saw my parents. They also were sleeping peacefully. I thought about my little sister and how I couldn't leave her, knowing that she loved me so much. I retuned back to my room, watching myself crying and shivering.

To travel around the house so freely was amazing. To walk through doors and walls was unbelievable. As I travelled back to my room, I remember seeing myself crying and it was like standing in front of the mirror looking at myself. Then, I saw my body starting to shake, then I stopped shaking. I also noticed that I was motionless. I thought to myself, "Did I die?". That's all I was asking myself, "Did I die? Did I die? I don't want to die, God. I'm too young. I just want someone to love me." I wasn't moving at all. My sister Ty came into the room and started shaking me over and over. When I saw her, my first thought was, "why is she in my room crying over that body lying there on the bed? I hovered over the lifeless body and then I noticed it was me!

I saw myself crying and taking my last breath. I watched myself just lying there. I regretted not telling my little sister that I loved her. At that moment I could hear my little sister's voice.

I fell right on myself, causing me to gasp for air and I started choking. I awoke not feeling the same, but really happy. Ty was so very happy that I woke up. I could feel this experience scared her so much. All I could do was hug her. I really didn't know what had happened. At least I told myself that! I told myself all the years that it was a dream—nothing more than a dream!

I woke up saying that it was just a bad dream, I kept saying that over and over to my sister so she would think I had a bad dream. I was confused and lost at that moment. Up until I looked in my sister's face the next morning, I didn't realize the impact that my choices or actions would have to the people that I loved. It just never occurred to me to think about how the people that I love would feel after I made those decisions.

This was my first out-of-body experience. When it happened, I was in denial. I would find myself in the same loveless moments again with my parents. Nothing changed. I still felt like I didn't have anyone. My girlfriend and I split up for good, Ty was still going through depression, and I really believe now that I was too. I just didn't know how to control it. My parents were on some other level at this point in time. Their love went two different ways. It was obvious that all of us were affected by the dynamics of the house. Some of the time we saw them love each other, and other times, they wouldn't even speak. I hated it! It confused me. It made me start to feel like I wanted to just die again. Would I be missed more dead or alive?

Invisible

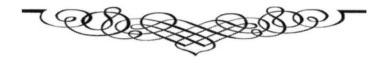

I had an after-school job working at Wendy's from 3:00 to 10:00 p.m. I wanted to work all night because I didn't want to go home. I wanted to just be away from the problems at home and I was just happier when I wasn't around the negativity at home and I began to have those thoughts again. If I die, would people cry? Would they love me more when I'm gone? I'd seen entertainers die, and fans would love them more. I would walk home thinking, "I'm going to jump off this bridge. I had already envisioned what was going to happen. I would jump off this bridge, get hit by the biggest truck, and wouldn't feel any pain. All the news media would cover the accident because I was a teenager. My parents would love me more if I was gone. I would be talked about every day. They would only think about the good times we had when I was a child. Everyone would be crying over my death, but they should have told me they loved me! That's all I wanted to hear, "I love you!" Why wait until I'm gone to say I love you, like so many people do? At that point I didn't care about what other people would feel because I couldn't feel anything, but pain and it took a lot for me to feel that. I was numb and invisible.

I got off of work early one day and with each step I took I was going over every moment of my life. All of the good moments came to mind first and it seemed so slow. Then all of the bad thoughts and memories came to mind. It was like I was trying to decide whether or not I was going to kill myself. Once I began to feel the weight of all of the negativity that comes with those thoughts, I just wanted to end it. It was almost as if something inside of me just clicked and in that moment, I made the decision to end my life. As I walked home, I thought to myself, if someone walks by me and doesn't speak, it will just prove that I was invisible and that I wasn't even worthy of them giving me eye contact. At that moment, I looked up and saw someone walking toward me. I didn't see where they came from, but as I looked back, I really don't know where they came from. As they passed me, they looked at me but they didn't speak. I couldn't tell if they were male or female. It was like they looked at me, but they didn't actually see me. I felt a strong vibration as they walked past me and I couldn't tell if the vibration was coming from the cars under the bridge or the person and everything felt like it was moving in slow motion. I was standing on the bridge watching the cars pass, I was thinking about how it would feel to jump in front of one of the vehicles. Would it hurt more because the cars were passing so slowly? I thought to myself, why is every car and truck going so slow? Even the wind and the

air stopped. The stars became brighter and each had a brilliant shine. The moon was so close, it felt like you could reach out and touch it. It was so close that I could see dips and craters in it. I walked toward the bridge and grabbed the rail. I could feel the vibrations again, but I couldn't explain what was happening at the moment because I was in denial that this could be something moving in the spirit.

    I stood up on the bridge and told myself I was going to jump. I jumped! All I saw was white! I felt a tug on my arm. Wow! That didn't hurt! Finally! No more school! No more problems! Just like that! I thought about my mother and how could I do that to her and my sisters? Are they going to hate me because I'm gone? I wanted to cry, but I couldn't because I just killed myself! What was I thinking??? All I wanted was love, that's all, and for someone to love me. I could hear my little sister, "Why did he kill himself? That's my big brother in that coffin. Why are there so many people here to see him in his coffin? Why is my mom crying so much? Why did big sister faint? Why would you do this, Big Brother? Why? I love you! I love you!". There were so many people all coming out to attend my funeral, but I didn't understand how so many people were showing up for me, but none of them did that while I was alive.

    Again, I heard my little sister's voice, "Why Big Brother? Why?". Then out of nowhere I started hearing a man's voice saying, "Why? You don't have to do this, Quest." As soon as I heard those words I started crying. I was completely distraught and overwhelmed with emotion.

    It was amazing for me to hear in that moment that someone cared enough about me to try and stop me. Then suddenly, I started to see a bright light. Hearing that voice and feeling the genuine concern about me felt amazing. I wondered where this voice of concern was coming from. I thought maybe it was a driver who had stopped and shined his high beams on me. The voice said, "Quest, come down. You don't have to do this!". I remember thinking, if I died, then why am I not in heaven yet?

Suddenly, I realized that I was back standing there on the ledge of the bridge, then I could hear my little sister's voice in my head again saying, "I love you, Big Brother!" I replied to the voice, "Who are you? How do you know my name? I thought I jumped. How did I get back up here?". "You didn't jump, Quest". I thought about it and realized that I did feel a tug after I jumped, but then the light was so bright around me that I couldn't make heads or tails of what had just happened. "No, Quest! I grabbed you in that moment. What you saw was your future flashing be- fore your eyes. You were considering what your mother might say when she finds out you killed yourself? Or how your dad might feel about you killing yourself?", right then I put my hand in front of my face to block the glare from the light shining in my face and I asked again, "Who are you? How do you know what I was thinking?", and the response was, "I know all about you, I'm here for you", but I shouted, "My dad doesn't love me! They don't love me! No one loves me! I don't want to live anymore because I'm not loved. I hurt so much inside because I want someone to love me. That's all." "I love you, Quest. Your sisters love you; your parents love you." He grabbed my arm and asked me to step down from the bridge.

"How do you know my name?" I asked. He put his hands on my shoulders and I could feel the warmth from his hands. It was as if he was reassuring me as he said, "You are loved,

Quest! From this day on you will be loved." When he said that, I stopped crying immediately. I turned around to see him face-to-face, but the light was so bright I could only see his silhouette. "Thank you for saving me because I almost jumped." Looking over the bridge, watching the biggest truck pass underneath, I said, "Wow! That would have hurt!". "You are loved, Quest," he reassured me again. As I looked away from the truck and back at him to ask him again how he knew my name he wasn't there! He'd vanished with the light that was shining so brightly in my face. It frightened me a little because as I looked up and down the street, there wasn't a car for miles around. I didn't know it then, but that was my first experience with an Angel. He was an angel. He knew everything about me and my family. I was kind of scared, so I started walking home, thinking about what had just happened to me. It was not a dream. You can't dream while you are awake. Why could I hear my little sister's voice? I ran home so fast it was unbelievable. I came into the house and went right to the bathroom. My heart was beating so fast. I threw water on my face. WOW! As I looked in the mirror, I noticed my pupils were huge so I tried to relax, closing my eyes and counting. When I opened my eyes again, my pupils were still enlarged. I heard a faint knock on the bathroom door so I opened it, and my little sister was standing there.

"What are you still doing up, Keisha?" I asked. She looked like she had been crying. I gave her a hug. "Big Brother, I had a bad dream about you. You're the best Big Brother in the world, and I don't want nothin' to happen to you." Now how could she have known what I just went through? Was she dreaming about what had really just happened to me? How? That was crazy!

The next morning, I wanted to tell everyone what had happened to me. I just didn't want to seem like a crazy person, so I didn't tell them about it until now.

Mirror

The reason the memory of my visit to heaven is so meaningful and powerful to me is because it is the one thing that anchored me to reality following a traumatic brain injury that I experienced. The accident that caused the injury had robbed me of everything, every memory and every one of my life experiences. I realized at that time that we are made up of more than just flesh and blood.

We are spiritual beings living in a physical world, but our spirits are made up of so much like our life experiences and the people that we love and care for. Following my accident, I was very angry with God, but I was grateful at the same time because he left me with that one amazing memory, and a sound mind and body. Now, God shows me my life and returns each memory as if I'm watching a movie and reliving every experience that makes me who I am. It's fascinating the way God is allowing me to recover my memories. Sometimes, I receive them in my dreams, sometimes I receive them in visions while I'm awake and it feels like they are so vivid that I feel like I'm reliving them all over again only with even more emotion because I understand so much more now. Can you imagine experiencing your life from a different perspective, as if you were watching your life in a mirror, as a spectator?

My Spiritual Dream

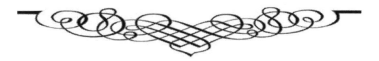

On February 17, 2009, 2:18 a.m., I woke up gasping for air. I started choking uncontrollably. I sat up on my bed and looked at my alarm clock. "2:18……..then 2:23… then 2:25*" I stood up and got a sip of water. I felt an emptiness in my heart for some reason. I put my hand over my heart and felt my heartbeat. It felt like I had two heartbeats; then it changed to one. I really felt different. I felt so alone! This feeling I was having, I couldn't explain. Maybe it was just a dream? But this dream felt too real because I could felt it deep in my soul. I felt like crying, but I didn't know why. I had been having the same dream for two weeks now. Maybe because I had been talking to my little sister, Keisha, every day. But this night, my dream was different. Every night I dreamt my little sister would be smiling, running toward me with her arms straight out, calling "Hey, Big Brother!", then I would grab her and throw her up in the air. But not this night, this night she would be smiling, running toward me with her arms straight out, calling "Hey, Big Brother," but this time she ran through me, never once looking back at me, as if she didn't need me anymore.

After that dream, my mind and soul were shaken. My thoughts were spinning around in my head so fast, like when you're a kid and an adult picks you up and spins you around in the air and places you on your feet . As I sat on the edge of my bed, visions of my little sister running through me over and over and over again kept repeating in my thoughts. I tried running after her, and grabbing her in the dream, but I couldn't. She was happy, smiling and laughing, with a flower in her hair and skipping off with this beautiful butterfly. As I stood there looking at her, I shouted her name, "Keisha! Come back! Where are you going? You can't leave me, Keisha!"

She skipped off again, but it wasn't a normal skip, it was a happy skip, more like getting candy from the Dollar Store! The butterfly made her more at peace. The butterfly first touched her hand, then it settled on her shoulder. It then flew around her as they went into the light. I felt joy and peace.

As I woke up, I was saddened because my little sis had run right through me. I couldn't move for a few minutes and I just sat there stunned and shocked. I couldn't even swallow normally. My heart was beating faster and faster and I kept asking myself if I was dreaming or not? My heart felt alone at that moment and I remember that the clock read 2:18 a.m. exactly. I sat at the edge of my bed for several minutes. I should have called her, but I didn't. I really should have called. Not making "that phone call" affects me to this day. I'm sure you're wondering "Why would it affect him like that?", but it was because if had I called my little Sis, she would have picked up the phone minutes before she died and maybe she wouldn't have died. That wasn't just a dream I had, it was real! It was her letting me know that she was okay and she didn't need Big Brotha to hold her hand anymore.

I didn't want to believe this or my dream, but it was true. Her spirit communicated with my spirit. There were so many moments in my dream that are just stained my brain. When I yelled for her, she just kept skipping. She never looked back at me. This dream by far is the worst dream of my life because it meant that I would really have to let her go, but it was also a beautiful moment because I knew that she was with God now. I had never had a dream where someone just passed right through me, especially a loved one, but if this ever happens to you, get up and call that person no matter what time it is. I often think about that "phone call." My little sis has communicated to me spiritually, "It's not your fault, Big Brother. God wanted me to come home. Don't sit here and cry over me. I'm okay, Big Brother. I'm okay now." I sat there, scared and in disbelief and I don't scare easily because of my professional training. I was scared because of the thought that if she didn't pick up, this was a demonstration of my gift of "knowing?" meaning being able to know when a person passes over. I really didn't know what to think. No one knows when my little sister took her last breath, not even the doctors, but I know in my heart that it was probably at 2:18 a.m. when it all happened.

What I also noticed from that dream were the surroundings. I remember that in my dream my little sis was skipping on the grass, which turned this real bright green and out of nowhere roses bloomed everywhere as her skip slowed down, each rose sparkled with love. God was giving me a glimpse of heaven showing me how it looked like a sneak preview. I didn't understand it then like I do now. Looking back on it now, I fully understand what I was seeing. My thoughts of heaven changed for good then. My day in heaven with my little sis will remain with me for the rest of my lifetime. When my mind is clear and I'm relaxed and free, I will take several deep breaths, close my eyes, and I can see heaven the way I did in my dream. I love it! One of my fondest memories is how Keisha would be the first one to call me and wish me happy birthday. On the night of my birthday, around 11:45 p.m. following Keisha's passing, I started to cry knowing I wouldn't hear my little sister's voice again and as tears rolled down my face, I thought back over the last twentynine years and how my little sis has always wished me a happy birthday every year. As I walked from my bedroom to the dining room with tears streaming down, I felt a "breeze" on my hands and face, but when I looked in the mirror I couldn't believe what I saw…there were absolutely no tears on my face! To this day, I believe that breeze wasn't just a breeze, but my little sis wiping away my sadness and tears. Then I heard her sweet voice say, "Happy birthday, Big Brother! I love you!" she whispered softly in my ear. "You thought you weren't ever going to hear my voice again, Big Brother, but how could I ever forget what day this is?" I was totally in shock, hearing her voice again, knowing she was there with me in that moment. It felt so real that I know I wasn't dreaming it.

  I know now that my life's purpose is to spread the love of God around the world. I want people to feel what I felt and envision what I've seen, having a clear understanding that if you show love, you will receive love. Everything in heaven that I've seen has been a blessing from God.

    I love and thank God so much for my experience. Having been given the experience of being in heaven makes me feel so loved joyful, and now my spirit is completely at peace.

Made in the USA
Columbia, SC
06 October 2020